The Future Stakes for U.S. Food and Agriculture in East and Southeast Asia

Steven A. Breth,
James A. Auerbach,
and Martha Lee Benz

Editors

Food and Agriculture Committee, National Policy Association
Foreign Agricultural Service, U.S. Department of Agriculture

**The Future Stakes for U.S. Food and Agriculture
in East and Southeast Asia**

NPA Report #291

Price: $15.00

ISBN 0-89068-146-5
Library of Congress
Card Catalog Number 98-89590

 29

The Future Stakes for U.S. Food and Agriculture in East and Southeast Asia

Steven A. Breth,
James A. Auerbach,
and Martha Lee Benz
Editors

PART V
THE SPECIAL CASE OF CHINA
AND ITS FUTURE DEVELOPMENT

PART VI
POLICIES TO AID U.S. FOOD AND AGRICULTURAL
TRADE AND INVESTMENT IN ASIA

CONCLUSION

About the Authors and Editors

Kevin D. Adams, Vice President, Zen-Noh Grain Corporation and Consolidated Grain and Barge Enterprises, Inc., is responsible for the commercial and operational aspects of the grain and woodchip export programs. Previously, he was Regional General Manager with Consolidated Grain and Barge Company and Merchandising Manager for Zen-Noh Grain Corporation and CGB Enterprises Inc.

John H. (Jack) Andre is Director of the Office of Economic Policy, Bureau of East Asian and Pacific Affairs, U.S. Department of State. He has also worked in the State Department's Office of Southern Cone Affairs, Inter-American Bureau, and in its Bureau of Economic and Business Affairs. Mr. Andre served as an economic officer in the U.S. Embassy in Manila, Philippines, and in Bangkok, Thailand.

James A. Auerbach is Senior Vice President of the National Policy Association. He is also Director of NPA's Food and Agriculture Committee and of the Committee on New American Realities, as well as Managing Editor of *Looking Ahead*, NPA's flagship quarterly journal. He has been an adjunct instructor at the University of Virginia and at the Foreign Affairs Training Institute, U.S. Department of State. Mr. Auerbach is Coeditor of *Through a Glass Darkly: Building the New Workplace for the 21st Century; The Inequality Paradox: Growth of Income Disparity;* and *Aging and Competition: Rebuilding the U.S. Workforce.*

Martha Lee Benz is Editor of the National Policy Association, including Editor of NPA's quarterly journal *Looking Ahead*. She has editorial responsibility for NPA's publications and has edited studies on wide-ranging topics such as seeds and world agricultural progress, the unique opportunities for the United States in Asia, emerging markets and international development, income inequality, aging and competition, and European and American labor markets.

Steven A. Breth is an independent editor and writer who specializes in agricultural issues. He was Editor of the Winrock Development-Oriented Literature Series published by Westview Press and is currently a Consulting Editor for the International Water Management Institute. Mr. Breth is author of *The Earth and the Sky* and Editor of *Agricultural Intensification in Sub-Saharan Africa* and *Women, Agricultural Intensification, and Household Food Security.*

Carole Brookins is Chairman and Chief Executive Officer of World Perspectives, Inc. Previously, she was Vice President in the Commodities Department of E.F. Hutton and Co., New York. She was Chair of the U.S. Department of State's private sector Advisory Committee on Food/Hunger and Agriculture in Developing Countries and was appointed by President Bush to the President's Export Council. Ms. Brookins is a member of the U.S. National Committee for Pacific Economic Cooperation Council and is currently Chair of the PECC Food and Agriculture Industry Forum.

William T. Coyle is Senior Economist, Asia-Western Hemisphere Branch, Economic Research Service, U.S. Department of Agriculture. His prior work with USDA includes heading the Asia initiative on prospects and impediments to agricultural trade in Asia; assisting in organization and program development for the Food and Agriculture Forums sponsored by the Pacific Economic Cooperation Council in 1994 and 1995; and Chief of the Developed Market Economies Branch.

Robert H. Curtis is Director, Agricultural Trade Office, American Embassy, Milan, Italy, and former Deputy Director of the Asia, Africa and Eastern Europe Division in the International Trade Policy area of the Foreign Agricultural Service, USDA. His overseas assignments have included Agricultural Attaché in Santiago, Chile, and Assistant Attaché in Buenos Aires, Argentina. Mr. Curtis has also worked in the FAS's Grain and Feed Division and in the Dairy, Livestock, and Poultry Division.

Dean A. DeRosa is Principal Economist of ADR International, Ltd. He has previously been an economist with the U.S. Department of the Treasury, the Asian Development Bank, and the International Monetary Fund, and a Research Fellow with the International Food Policy Research Institute. He has contributed numerous articles on international trade and protection to economic journals and other publications.

Mark R. Drabenstott, Vice President and Economist at the Federal Reserve Bank of Kansas City, is responsible for overseeing research on the bank's seven-state Tenth Federal Reserve District. He is a widely noted author and speaker on topics such as farm policy, agricultural trade, rural and economic development, and the food industry. Dr. Drabenstott is Chair of NPA's Food and Agriculture Committee and a Director of the National Bureau of Economic Research.

Michael J. Dwyer is International Economist, Commodity and Marketing Programs, Foreign Agricultural Service, USDA. He is responsible for strategic marketing analyses of U.S. and world agricultural trade, global competitiveness, and trade forecasting. He previously served as coordinator of the Agricultural Information and Marketing Services Project for FAS, the forerunner of *AgExport Connections*. Mr. Dwyer has authored a number of studies assessing the effectiveness of export promotion activities on U.S. agricultural exports.

John Dyck is Team Leader in the Asia-Western Hemisphere Branch, Economic Research Service, USDA. He coordinates economic reporting and analysis on Asia's agriculture, food consumption, and agricultural trade and is also an analyst for Northeast Asia. Since joining ERS in 1979, he has also served as analyst for Thailand, North and South Korea, and Japan.

Richard Gilmore is President and Chief Executive Officer of GIC Trade, Inc. Formerly Chief Economist of the U.S. Senate Committee on Foreign Relations, he is an advisor to government agencies on agricultural issues and a member of the Council on Foreign Relations. Dr. Gilmore has also served as a Fellow with the Rockefeller Foundation and the Rand Corporation and as an agricultural commentator for CNN. He has been a Guest Scholar at the Overseas Development Council and a Senior Project Director for Food Issues at the Carnegie Endowment for International Peace.

Christopher E. Goldthwait is General Sales Manager of the USDA's Foreign Agricultural Service and Vice President of the Commodity Credit Corporation. He administers foreign market development activities, export credit activities, and PL 480 (Food for Peace Program), oversees the Export Enhancement Program, and is responsible for direct sales of surplus commodities into export markets. Since joining FAS in 1973, Mr. Goldthwait has held a variety of positions, including Management Analyst, Deputy Assistant Administrator for International Agricultural Statistics, and Agricultural Counselor in Lagos, Nigeria.

Dale E. Hathaway is Director and Senior Fellow of the National Center for Food and Agricultural Policy. He was on the White House staff of Presidents Eisenhower's and Kennedy's Council of Economic Advisors and was UnderSecretary of Agriculture for International Affairs and Commodity Programs from 1977 to 1981. He was Chief Negotiator on Agricultural Issues in the Tokyo Round of the GATT, served on the Transition Team for Agriculture for the Clinton administration, and is currently Chair of the Agricultural Policy Advisory Committee. Dr. Hathaway is the author of numerous books, articles, and monographs on agricultural policies and international trade.

Erland Heginbotham is former Chief, China Agricultural Strategy Project, Institute for Global Chinese Affairs, University of Maryland at College Park. He has been a Senior Fellow at the National Policy Association and Director of Gateway Japan. He earlier served as Director, Office of Industries of the U.S. International Trade Commission, senior staff member, U.S. Senate Committee on Foreign Relations, and Deputy Assistant Secretary of State, Bureau of East Asia and Pacific Affairs. He is the author of *Asia's Rising Economic Tide: Unique Opportunities for the U.S.* and numerous studies on Asian economics.

Robbin S. Johnson was elected Corporate Vice President, Public Affairs, Cargill, Incorporated, in 1993. He is a member of Cargill's Management Operating Committee, Chair of the Contributions Committee, and Vice Chair of the Public Affairs Committee. Mr. Johnson is also on the board of the Cargill Foundation. He serves on the boards of the International Policy Council on Agriculture and Trade and the National Center for the Asia-Pacific Economic Cooperation forum. He is a past Chair of the U.S. Feed Grains Council and is a member of the Council on Foreign Relations.

Christopher B. Johnstone is a Research Fellow at the Asia Pacific Center for Security Studies. Previously, he was Government Relations Analyst, Japan Economic Institute of America. He has also worked for Senator Hiroshi Ohki, National Diet, Tokyo, Japan; for the Trade and Economic Policy section, U.S. Embassy in Tokyo; and in the Japan Exchange and Teaching Program in Yokohama, Japan.

Earl D. Kellogg is Associate Provost, International Affairs, and Professor of Agricultural and Consumer Economics, University of Illinois at Urbana-Champaign. Previously, he was Senior Vice President and Chief Operating Officer, Winrock International Institute for Agricultural Development. Dr. Kellogg has been a special consultant to the U.S. Secretary of Agriculture's office and has had consulting assignments for numerous international and domestic institutions, including the U.S. Agency for International Development, the Food and Agriculture Organization of the United Nations, and the governments of Bahrain and Brazil. He has written more than 80 publications on agricultural and rural development.

William F. Kuckuck is President of International Sales of Tyson Foods, Inc. He previously served as Vice President and Managing Director, Asia Pacific Region, Tyson Foods International, and as Vice President and Chief Operating Officer, Asia Pacific Operations, Ralston Purina International. Currently, Mr. Kuckuck is Chair of Tyson Foods International Holding Company and Executive Director, United States of America Poultry and Egg Export Council. He has served as Chair of the Canadian Feed Industry Association and as Chair of the Community Relations Committee, American Chamber of Commerce-Hong Kong.

Nicholas R. Lardy is a Senior Fellow in Foreign Policy Studies at The Brookings Institution. Previously, he was Director of the Henry M. Jackson School of International Studies, Professor of International Studies, and Chair of the China Program at the University of Washington. He has been a Professor of Economics and Assistant Director of the Economic Growth Center at Yale University. Dr. Lardy is the author of *China in the World Economy* as well as numerous articles and books on the Chinese economy. He serves on the Board and Executive Committee of the National Committee on United States-China Relations.

Will Martin is Principal Economist in the World Bank's Development Research Group specializing in international economics. He uses econometric and simulation models to help understand the fundamental influences on trade and development, with much of his current research focusing on Asia. Prior to joining the World Bank, Dr. Martin held research and management positions at the Australian Bureau of Agriculture and Resource Economics and was a Senior Research Fellow at the Australian National University.

Edward E. Masters is President of the United States-Indonesia Society. His previous positions include U.S. Ambassador to Indonesia and Bangladesh and Deputy Chief of Mission in Thailand; Senior Vice President, International Affairs, Natomas Company;

Adjunct Professor, Asian Studies, Fletcher School of Law and Diplomacy; and President and Chief Executive Officer of the National Policy Association. He achieved the senior rank of Career Minister at the U.S. Department of State, where he had also been Director of the Office of East Asian Regional Affairs. He has been decorated by the government of Indonesia for his contributions to improving U.S.-Indonesian relations.

Paul Morris is Minister-Counsellor for Agriculture and Resources at the Australian Embassy, Washington, D.C. Mr. Morris spent 12 years in the Australian Bureau of Agricultural and Resource Economics of the Department of Primary Industries and Energy. He has also worked on the secretariat of three government inquiries: the Royal Commission into Grain Storage, Handling and Transport; the Committee of Review into the Wool Industry; and the Wool Industry Review Committee. Mr. Morris was Australia's representative to the Organization for Economic Cooperation and Development Committee for Fisheries in 1993 and 1994.

Sherman Robinson is Director of the Trade and Macroeconomics Division, International Food Policy Research Institute. From 1983 to 1995, he was a Professor in the Department of Agricultural and Resource Economics, University of California at Berkeley. He has served as Division Chief in the Research Department of the World Bank and as a Senior Economist with the Council of Economic Advisors. Dr. Robinson has also worked at the Economic Research Service, USDA, and was an Assistant Professor of Economics at Princeton University. He has published numerous books and articles on trade policy, the economics of developing countries as well as socialist states, and environmental and agricultural sector models.

R. Gerald (Jerry) Saylor is Director of Market Economics and former Manager of Agricultural Economic Research at Deere & Company. Previously, Mr. Saylor has worked for the Ford Foundation in São Paulo, Brazil, and Cairo, Egypt, and for the Economics Research Bureau in Tanzania, East Africa. He has been an Assistant Professor at Michigan State University and a Research Economist at the Federal Reserve Bank of Dallas.

Douglas A. Scott is an international economist specializing in economic development and reform of the instruments and institutions for macroeconomic management. From 1967 until his retirement in 1996, Dr. Scott was employed by the International Monetary Fund in positions that included IMF Resident Representative in Beijing, China, and Jakarta, Indonesia, and Deputy Director of the IMF Central Banking Department. Prior to joining the IMF, Dr. Scott was an MIT Fellow-in-Africa in Uganda and Ghana.

T.C. Tso is Chairman of the Board of the Institute of International Development and Education in Agriculture and Life Sciences, Inc. (IDEALS), where he has worked since 1984, following his retirement from the Agricultural Research Service, USDA. Previously, Mr. Tso was an Affiliate Professor in the Agronomy Department, University of Maryland. In 1983, he was conferred the Rank of Meritorious Executive of the U.S. Senior Executive Service by President Reagan. Mr. Tso continues to serve as Collaborator, National Program Staff, ARS, USDA.

Wan Baouri has been Vice Minister of Agriculture, People's Republic of China, since 1993. He has worked in the Ministry of Agriculture since 1987, in the Department of General Planning as Deputy Director-General and Research Fellow and later as Director-General.

Charles F. Weden, Jr., is a former Deputy Assistant Administrator, Bureau for Asia and the Near East, U.S. Agency for International Development. He also served as USAID's Associate Director for Programs in Egypt; Director in Yemen; Director in Tunisia; Deputy Assistant Administrator for the Near East Bureau; and Director in Indonesia.

Kaoru Yoshimura is former Agricultural Counselor, Embassy of Japan in Washington, D.C. Previously, Mr. Yoshimura held positions in the Ministry of Agriculture, Forestry, and Fisheries in Japan and in the Ministry of Finance. Topics of Mr. Yoshimura's prior publications include agriculture in urbanized areas and the green field system and policies for rationalizing farm land possession.

Acknowledgments

Food and Agriculture Committee (FAC) members wish to express our appreciation to the contributors to this book. Our thanks to those who assisted in the preparation of the manuscript: James A. Auerbach, FAC Director, who oversaw the preparation of the monograph, and Steven A. Breth, manuscript editor, Martha Lee Benz, NPA Editor, and Laura E. Juhnke, NPA Editorial Assistant, for their critical roles in assuring clarity and cohesion, as well as meticulous copy editing.

Finally, this book would not have been possible without the support provided by the Foreign Agricultural Service of the U.S. Department of Agriculture; Cargill, Incorporated; Dow AgroSciences; The Farm Foundation; McDonald's Corporation; Pioneer Hi-Bred International, Inc.; and the United Food and Commercial Workers International Union, AFL-CIO.

INTRODUCTION

Reaching for the Asian Food Market: Prerequisites for Progress

by Mark R. Drabenstott

*Vice President and Economist,
Federal Reserve Bank of Kansas City,
and Chair, NPA Food and Agriculture Committee*

Asia, already the largest buyer of U.S. farm and food exports, holds greater promise for U.S. food and agriculture than any other region in the world. From Japan and South Korea in the north to Indonesia and Malaysia in the south and finally to China, the East and Southeast Asia region is the world's largest marketplace for food. The region has 1.9 billion people, and population is growing rapidly in many countries. Even more important, rising incomes are fueling a dramatic upgrading of diets. To satisfy its growing appetite for food in the 1990s, the region has turned to world markets and major food exporters such as the United States. Despite the region's recent economic turmoil, some analysts still believe that U.S. food exports to the region could grow by one-half over the coming decade.

Clearly, the U.S. food and agricultural sector has enormous stakes in East and Southeast Asia. But the potential will not develop automatically. The serious financial crisis throughout the region underscores the point. The Asian food market will reach its vast potential only in a policy environment that fosters steady economic growth, stronger trade ties, and new capital investment.

Recognizing Asia's potential for U.S. food and agriculture and the policy prerequisites for reaching that potential, the Food and Agriculture Committee (FAC) of the National Policy Association undertook this book. Over the course of more than two years, the Committee commissioned 27 presentations, made at several FAC meetings, on the Asian food market and the policies needed to realize its vast potential. This book presents the findings of these experts, who revised and updated in late 1998.

The Committee's examination of the Asian food market led to three main findings, summarized in this introductory chapter.

- The U.S. food and agricultural industry truly has big stakes in Asia—the potential is vast and largely unrealized.

- Policies that free trade and foster steady economic growth are keys to unlocking the potential in the Asian food market.

- Changes in U.S. development assistance would help U.S. firms boost sales to the region.

1

THE HUGE STAKES IN ASIA FOR U.S. FOOD AND AGRICULTURE

There is strong consensus that East and Southeast Asia represent big food markets today and even bigger markets tomorrow. The region offers a prime example of the best formula for boosting food demand: Add rapid income gains to a large and growing population. While this formula is also at work in Latin America and, to a lesser extent, eastern Europe, no part of the world economy offers more upside potential in food demand than Asia.

Before looking ahead, it is useful to recognize that Asia has already had a major impact on U.S. food exports. A decade ago, the East and Southeast Asian countries accounted for about 33 percent of U.S. agricultural exports (Figure 1). Today, that share is almost 40 percent. Japan has remained an important market throughout the period, but the major increases have occurred in countries where economic growth has lifted incomes and consumers have stepped up food purchases. China, for example, was a marginal customer of U.S. food and agriculture 10 years ago, but after a decade of exceptional economic growth, China is now the U.S.'s seventh biggest single-country market. With similar kinds of economic gains elsewhere in the region, Asia has quickly become the dominant customer for U.S. food and agriculture.

The potential is even greater. Further population growth will be a key factor in raising food demand in Asia. With the exception of China, the population of the region is expected to grow faster than the world average

FIGURE 1
DESTINATION OF U.S. AGRICULTURAL EXPORTS, 1986 AND 1996

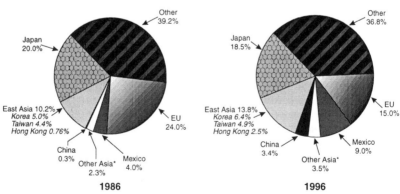

*Other Asia includes Indonesia, Malaysia, Philippines, and Thailand.

Source: FAS, USDA.

FIGURE 2

DEVELOPMENT OF THE WORLD FOOD SYSTEM: FOOD PRODUCTION PER CAPITA IN RELATION TO GNP PER CAPITA

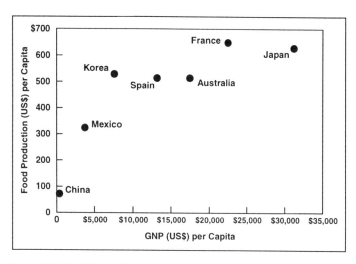

Source: IMF, *World Economic Outlook.*

of 1.4 percent a year through 2005, meaning that Asia's population growth will run far ahead of the slight gains in population in the developed world.

Income growth will be an even larger factor in boosting food demand across Asia. Per capita incomes remain low in many Asian nations, pointing to large potential gains in food consumption when incomes begin to rise. When incomes are low, a substantial portion of the average diet is often produced at home, and the minimal quantities purchased are generally raw or unprocessed foods. In China, for instance, per capita incomes average less than $500* per year, and per capita production in the food system is only $70 a year (Figure 2).

With rising incomes, however, food systems become more developed as consumers spend more on processed foods. In Japan, a nation with one of the world's highest living standards, per capita income tops $30,000 a year, and per capita production in the food system exceeds $600. With higher incomes, spending rises first for foods in which processing has added relatively little value, such as processed fats and oils, meats, and dairy products. As incomes rise still further, consumers can afford more highly

---

*Unless otherwise noted, all monetary amounts throughout this book are in current U.S. dollars.

processed products, such as precooked and packaged foods. In short, rising incomes tend to tilt food demand from bulk commodities to processed food products. The U.S. food and agricultural sector can benefit in many ways from this scenario of rising food consumption. It can sell more food-processing technology to Asian companies. It can sell more bulk commodities to supply a growing Asian food system. It can sell more finished, higher margin food products to Asian food retailers. Alternatively, it can invest in new food-processing or food-retailing ventures in the region. Taken together, this is a rich menu of opportunities for U.S. food and agriculture. Because this vital sector accounts for almost one-sixth of U.S. gross domestic product, it will also provide significant benefits to the U.S. economy and the U.S. trade balance.

Recent financial market turmoil will clearly impede Asian economies over the next few years, slowing the growth of, or perhaps reducing, food imports from the United States and other food-exporting countries. How long this slowdown persists will depend to a considerable extent on how policymakers in the region respond. Once this period is past, however, the long-term fundamentals still point to the vast potential for the United States to sell substantially more food in Asia.

POLICY PREREQUISITES FOR THE ASIAN FOOD MARKET

The recent financial crisis across East and Southeast Asia underscores the need for a sound policy framework to realize the great potential of the Asian food market. This policy framework appears to have two linchpins—trade policy and stable economic policy. Both will serve the interests of U.S. food and agriculture.

The Asian food market should be built squarely on policies that promote free trade. Viewed in simple terms, a rising tide of food and agricultural products will need to cross many borders to satisfy the region's growing appetite for food imports. What is more, the region will need to sell a panoply of products and services in world markets to buy U.S. food. In short, U.S. food sales to the region depend on a reliable set of trade policies that promote free commerce in both directions.

Few industries have a larger stake in pushing for free trade worldwide than U.S. food and agriculture. Indeed, U.S. agriculture was a major proponent of the Uruguay Round of the General Agreement on Tariffs and Trade. In that round, U.S. agriculture made considerable efforts to eliminate farm and trade subsidies in Europe and elsewhere. Yet, many of the Uruguay Round's benefits to the industry have come not from the relatively modest reductions in agricultural trade barriers achieved there; rather, the benefits derive from the swelling of trade that flows from tariff reductions in the other 14 product categories. Cutting European Union export subsidies a billion dollars here and there will provide some modest gains in U.S. agricultural sales abroad. But adding trillions of dollars to the global economy will produce a large, sustained rise in global food demand and U.S. food exports.

Thus, the U.S. food and agricultural sector stands to gain enormously from efforts to promote free trade throughout the Pacific Rim. Strong efforts will be needed in dealing with the major challenges that lie ahead. Fast track authority is needed in the United States to spur new rounds of talks. Discussion of China's accession to the World Trade Organization will be a central issue in ensuring free trade in the region. Attention will need to focus on trade in genetically modified organisms. U.S. firms will want reassurances that their research investments in the region will be protected from infringement. U.S. firms will also want to be able to bring unique genetic and research products from Asia to the United States and other parts of the globe.

Sound economic policy will be the other linchpin of progress in the Asian food market. Scores of millions of Asian people are on the threshold of major dietary improvement. Vigorous economic growth will be the key to helping them move up the food ladder. Sound economic policy will likely include two crucial components. First, the region will need macroeconomic policies that avoid both inflation and economic imbalances. Many countries in the region have been effective in holding inflation at levels low enough to sustain economic growth. While some countries may be tempted to inflate their way out of banking and financial problems, such a course ultimately has disastrous effects on consumer welfare. Even if Asian policymakers are tempted, foreign exchange markets are likely to discourage them from pursuing inflationary policies.

Second, the countries of East and Southeast Asia will need sound financial systems to support investment throughout the region. Many countries will need to make massive investments in domestic infrastructure to support growing food imports from the United States. In China, for instance, new ports and railroads are badly needed to move food from coastal cities to inland population centers. These infrastructure investments simply will not be made if the banking and financial systems are unstable. Thus, U.S. agriculture has much to gain from current efforts by the International Monetary Fund and other institutions to restore financial stability throughout the region.

RETHINKING U.S. DEVELOPMENT ASSISTANCE

The United States may be missing an opportunity to gain full access to the Asian food market. Compared with the vast potential the Asian food market represents for the U.S. food and agricultural sector, U.S. development assistance to the region seems alarmingly low. Experts in agricultural assistance agree that additional aid would open new doors to a huge market.

Historically, development assistance has been an important means for developing new markets for U.S. agriculture. This assistance has ranged from the Food for Peace Program (PL 480) to the U.S. Agency for International Development (USAID) programs. As a helping hand to developing countries, the programs enable countries to modernize agricultural production and make the transition to a more industrialized economy. In the process, incomes in the countries rise, diets improve, and food demand grows significantly, opening new markets for U.S. export sales.

South Korea provides a good example. After the Korean War, it was the recipient of PL 480 food donations and then a stream of USAID projects. Over time, South Korean agriculture increased its productivity substantially, but the gains were far outstripped by the increasing food demand as the South Korean economy grew. Thus, the volume of food imports, much of which was from the United States, expanded rapidly. Today, South Korea is the fourth largest market for U.S. food and agricultural exports.

Despite the benefits of U.S. development assistance, U.S. efforts in Asia have been declining. Today, assistance to the region totals a mere $151 million a year, roughly one-third of the amount the United States spent in 1990 and an even smaller fraction of its spending two decades ago. Moreover, Asian development assistance appears out of line with the potential the region holds. Asian spending, for instance, accounts for just 5 percent of total USAID spending abroad, yet the region looms much larger as a potential trading partner. The region's need for development assistance is certainly less than it once was due to its economic progress over the past several years. Nevertheless, experts believe that significant opportunities still exist to provide assistance that will serve U.S. commercial interests in the long run.

CONCLUSIONS

U.S. food and agriculture has huge stakes in East and Southeast Asia. The region already represents the single biggest market for the industry's broad array of food sales abroad, and it has an even greater potential. Yet that potential will not come automatically, as the recent financial crisis amply demonstrates. Freer trade and sound economic policies will be policy prerequisites to a growing Asian food market. Moreover, after cutbacks in U.S. development assistance this decade, many now believe that U.S. aid could play a larger role in complementing the region's own growth agenda. While U.S. food and agriculture represent a large, diverse sector that spans input providers to food retailers, the chapters in this book clearly show that the industry will be a sturdy advocate of the policies that promote a brighter economic future in this vital region of the world.

PART I

OPPORTUNITIES FOR U.S. FOOD AND AGRICULTURE IN ASIA

1

Agricultural Trade Among Pacific Rim Countries

by Carole Brookins

*Chairman and Chief Executive Officer,
World Perspectives, Inc.*

T his chapter's discussion of the potential for food and agricultural trade in Asia centers on the countries of the Pacific Rim. It is important to realize that the United States is part of this region. Pacific Rim trade means intraregional trade. The United States benefits from being an Atlantic trading power, a Pacific trading power, and a hemispheric trading power. Pacific Rim trade with East and Southeast Asia brings the United States into markets that over the past decade have experienced the world's most dynamic growth and will again.

MAJOR FACTORS OF MARKETS

Four major factors—population, purchasing power, policy/politics, and participation—should be considered in analyzing world agricultural and food markets. In the case of the Pacific Rim, all of these factors are crucial in determining the potential for consumer demand growth and how that demand will be met within the food system.

Population

The Pacific Rim is vast; it includes the United States, Canada, the west coast of Latin America, all of Northeast and Southeast Asia, Russia, and the links to the Indian subcontinent. The consuming public of this region totals almost 75 percent of the world's population. Even excluding the Indian subcontinent, the Pacific Rim still encompasses 50 percent of the world's people.

Demographics show an astounding force within the large population of East and Southeast Asia. In the emerging countries, more than 30 percent of the consumers are under 15 years of age. In addition, the Asia-Pacific region has a strong population growth rate overall, and 9 of the world's 14 current "mega-cities" of more than 10 million people are in Asia. By 2015, 7 out of 10 of the world's cities with over 20 million inhabitants are estimated to be in Asia, and 17 more are projected to have populations between 10 million and 20 million. These "supermarkets" and "hypermarkets" will have unprecedented food requirements, which will have a tremendous impact on trade and investment in the food system.

Further, in most emerging Pacific Rim market economies, as much as 75 percent of the population still live in rural areas. As wealth expands, they will join the ranks of urban consumers in developing their incomes and taste for a wider variety of high quality food products in their diets.

Purchasing Power

No one in 1996 forecast the potential magnitude of the Asian markets' collapse. In fact, the emerging markets of Asia were widely viewed as the successful result of a commitment toward market capitalism. Global speculators' attack on the Thai baht in July 1997 opened up the deep crevice of global market investor confidence in how Asian companies and governments had managed their financial affairs. This in turn triggered a run on currencies and resulted in bankrupting governments, major corporations, and small and medium-sized businesses in several crisis countries. The financial crisis was worsened by the initial efforts of the International Monetary Fund (IMF) to stabilize financial markets by using policy prescriptions that had worked in reforming Latin America's state-controlled economies in the 1980s, but that were unsuitable in the Asian situation. By the end of 1997, it was apparent that the depth of economic decay was far more serious than had initially been estimated and that the timeframe for recovery was going to be far longer and require many more resources than had previously been projected. In the case of agricultural/food product trade, the Asian markets have been constrained by the lack of purchasing power by individuals and by the lack of foreign exchange by importers.

This tragedy has serious implications for global trade and for the world's economic performance. More important, the harsh impacts of financial restructuring, and in some cases economic depression, have wiped out as much as a decade of gross domestic product (GDP) growth, reversed the rising tide of aspiring middle class consumers, and pushed huge numbers of people below the poverty line.

Although the financial crisis does not mean that the "glow" is off the Asian markets, it does mean that over the short term several negative impacts will slow the growth in food trade and demand.

- Deflationary factors are affecting not only agricultural commodities but all commodity markets.

- Commercial sales are requiring financing support through government credit guarantees, and rising poverty levels are triggering expanded demand for food donations and assistance.

- Countries that had freely imported food from abroad when their currencies were pegged to the U.S. dollar have seen the cost of food imports rise by as much as 80 percent from pre-crisis levels. This will give greater credibility to proponents of food self-sufficiency policies.

- Both private and public sector investment in the food system's infrastructure is falling behind.

- With massive unemployment, the strong labor demands of industries in urban areas are being reversed, and the urbanization trend is slowing as people are moving back to the countryside in the hope of surviving through subsistence agriculture.

The resulting recession to depression conditions forecast through 1999 and the plunge in asset values mean that recovery will not be immediate and that political instability, labor unrest, and social turmoil will continue during the adjustment period. Regaining market growth will require substantial restructuring of governments, financial systems, trade and investment regimes, and corporate governance.

However, Asia-Pacific will begin to recover from the financial crisis by the end of 1999. From that point, the region could well assume a more solid and dynamic growth track than previously. Asia has the potential to control as much as 50 percent of global GDP by 2025. The U.S. share of global GDP in 2025 is forecast to remain at its current level, while Latin America's share is expected to rise by several percentage points. If this forecast is correct, Europe will be the loser in its share of the world economy.

Under this scenario for Asian recovery, the good news for the longer term may lie in today's bad economic news—that is, the harsh restructuring necessary today is likely to produce an even stronger marketplace in the early 21st century. Putting Asia back on the track of global market growth will require changes in the way that private and public officials do business. Reforms under way will:

- accelerate integration and globalization of markets;

- improve market transparency;

- set international standards for corporate management;

- improve governance of public and private financial institutions;

- shift private capital flows from portfolio investment and bank lending to direct equity investment; and

- reduce barriers to investment.

Over the next five years, East Asia is not expected to recover the 8.5 percent annual compound growth achieved during the past decade, which came to a stunning halt and reversal in mid-1997. Pre-crisis, East Asia captured more than 60 percent of the world's private capital flows to developing countries, and the domestic savings rate in each country averaged about 35 percent of GDP. Asian savings is a cultural tradition, with Japan alone accounting for one-half of the world's total savings. As the Asian recovery advances, the countries will again attract foreign direct investment (FDI). The positive turnaround in Fall 1998 in Asian equity markets was a sign of resurgence in consumer confidence. Foreign investors are hungrily looking to buy ownership in Asian businesses at bargain rates. Economic recovery will help support a recovery in indigenous investment/savings to fuel development. The United States is in a unique strategic position to access the future demand of more potential buyers as well as the more effective and sustainable buying power on the upswing at the turn of the 21st century.

Policy/Politics

In considering U.S. agrifood trade in the Pacific Rim, potential macroeconomic developments should be examined as well as intraregional trade flows and factors shaping the marketplace for food products. Intraregional trade has grown as a share of total Asian trade. Intraregional trade in food and agricultural products accounted for more than 60 percent of total trade by Pacific Rim countries in 1996, up from 30 percent in 1980.

The Pacific Rim stands to again provide tremendous opportunities for agriculture, with East and Southeast Asia large net importers of food products and North America, Australia, and New Zealand large net exporters. In fact, before the crisis of 1997, East Asia was the largest importing region of agricultural products in the world and despite the crisis, retains this standing.

The U.S. agrifood system has a large comparative advantage in the Pacific Rim because of the natural endowments of the United States (land, water, and climate), energy advances, low cost commodity production, efficient marketing, transportation structure, and leadership in utilizing innovative food system technology. The U.S. advantage is multiplied by technological leadership in production such as advanced genetics and competitive telecommunication systems, including global positioning satellites that improve production. Downstream, the United States has advanced tracking and marketing systems for consumer-ready food products. The United States, unlike Europe, is encouraging advanced production technology such as biotechnology.

Agriculture should therefore be at the forefront of U.S. efforts to open markets and not be put on the back burner in trade fights that erupt with Asian countries over issues such as telecommunications, automobiles, and other manufactured products. The agrifood system is one of the most important and successful high technology exports of the United States, and this fact should be made clear to the administration and Congress.

People buy food first. Although consumers in the United States spend roughly 10 percent of their disposable income on food, consumers in Europe spend 18 to 24 percent, in Japan, 25 percent, and in South Korea, 30 percent. This means that U.S. overseas customers have less money to buy, for example, telephones from MCI or airplanes from Boeing. Agricultural proponents do not talk about this. They usually say that agriculture is 20 percent of U.S. GDP and 20 percent of jobs. But these percentages do not begin to take into account the multiplier effect of agriculture on the U.S. economy. This is an important point particularly in dealing with the significant food and agricultural markets of the Pacific Rim countries.

In fact, the importance of Asian markets cannot be overstated. Total U.S. exports to Asia surged 40 percent between 1995 and 1997 to almost $200 billion, of which more than $20 billion were agricultural exports. In 1996, 60 percent of all U.S. exports—a record $33 billion—went to the countries of the Asia-Pacific Economic Cooperation (APEC) forum. Although much of that was related to trade with Mexico and Canada, more than 40 percent went to the Asia-Pacific market. Seventy-five percent of all U.S. consumer food exports go to APEC countries.

Since the financial crisis and the deflationary impact on agricultural prices and markets, some U.S. farmers, ranchers, and food processors have faced sharply lower earnings. Thus, it is in the U.S. national interest that Asia's economic growth engine be put back on track.

However, this may be made even more difficult because Asian governments will be less confident in market-opening negotiations. They will be trying much harder to protect their farmers and rural residents from competition, as they attempt to build their food production and export capabilities. Asian countries cannot be expected to concede to U.S. demands for unlimited access to their consumers until they regain confidence in their own economic viability and in their capacity to protect their people from another severe shock from global markets.

With this in mind, the United States must maintain a focus on trade liberalization in the agrifood sector and in bilateral, regional, and multilateral negotiations. To fully capitalize on the obvious advantages of the United States and build markets for U.S. agrifood exporters and investors in Asia, U.S. policymakers should address five key issues.

1. Liberalization

Market access is crucial, and the Uruguay Round of the General Agreement on Tariffs and Trade (GATT) was only the beginning of a long process to reduce tariffs and nontariff barriers and to open markets for U.S. farm and food products. In APEC, agriculture must be kept as a regular annual deliverable and not considered too difficult or sensitive to deal with until 2010 or 2020, when trade in APEC is to be completely liberalized. Several steps could be taken, in addition to pressing for sensitive accelerated tariff rate reductions. The United States must continue to focus on realistic goals, such as bringing greater consensus to regulatory standards even if short-term tariff cuts cannot be accelerated.

In advancing the U.S. agenda, it is important to remember that Asians have a different approach to negotiating. It is possible to make considerable progress in gaining consensus on sensitive issues if people understand that there are mutual benefits. For example, China should be brought into the

World Trade Organization (WTO) and be helped to understand that if it has more transparent standards, its exporters will benefit, whereas China sees transparent standards as making the country vulnerable to imports. The Chinese, particularly in the southern provinces, want to be players in the fruit and vegetable export market. The United States needs to link these objectives in a trade package and bring together food industry officials (such as those in the refrigeration industry) to build the sector. This approach differs from banging on the table and saying, "You must do it our way. It is the only right way." In a sense, U.S. negotiators have to become less American.

In considering trade and investment liberalization, agricultural interests in the United States have too narrow a perspective. Whether it is in APEC or the WTO, agriculture must become engaged as a mainstream industry participant in all negotiating groups. Agriculture should not be treated as separate from the rest of the economy, but as an integral part of many other issues, including investment, intellectual property rights, information technologies, financial services, the environment, and maritime services. As food and agricultural trade and investment are again opened up in the Pacific Rim, U.S. agriculture must be part of the mainstream in all these areas.

2. Nontariff Barriers

The second issue is nontariff barriers such as sanitary and phytosanitary (SPS) rules. The most important agreement negotiated during the Uruguay Round may have been the SPS agreement. A new era of technology and science is beginning, and the SPS agreement sets the framework and the precedent for negotiating environmental and other standards rules. With sound science now included as part of the SPS rules, real progress can be made in reducing nontariff barriers in the WTO.

In every negotiation, the importance of regulatory reform and harmonization must be advanced. Because the word "harmonization" frightens many Asians, the terms "process similarities" or "market similarities" are used instead. Regardless, mutual recognition agreements in the agrifood sector should be developed to the extent possible in standards, inspection, and processes.

3. Biotechnology

Nowhere could SPS rules hurt the future of U.S. food exports more than in the new scientific area of biotechnology. Each year attempts are made to liberalize trade in APEC, but there is opposition to reducing tariffs. With biotechnology regulations currently at an early stage in many countries, perhaps the APEC economies could agree to negotiate a mutual recognition agreement in biotechnology. A consensus in APEC could be carried to other regions. Given that several APEC members are also part of the negotiations for a Free Trade Agreement of the Americas, the same process could take place in those negotiations and then be carried to global negotiations.

4. A "Reliable-Exporter" Pledge

The negotiation of a reliable-exporter pledge, or nondiscrimination clause, should be given priority. Nondiscrimination between domestic and overseas buyers in times of short supply should be formally committed in APEC and the WTO. Many in Asia believe that they should become self-sufficient and self-reliant because of the short supply in 1995-97. The United States remained a reliable supplier during that period, but Europe imposed export taxes, and Canada imposed an allocation system.

I have proposed a "Golden Rule" commitment to nondiscrimination in the WTO. The language in the Uruguay Round agreement under Article 12, which sets the rules for export prohibitions and restrictions, should be strengthened. Even though the United States has set forth positive language, it has not made the commitment official. Many are concerned about what would happen if the United States actually had short supply and whether its domestic industries would be protected. However, under a nondiscrimination clause, supply would be allocated regardless; if supply has to be allocated, no one wants to shut off foreign buyers who are U.S. growth markets. As part of the Pacific Rim, the United States should advance this clause as a major part of APEC's 1999 agenda.

5. U.S. Strategic Interests

The U.S. status as a reliable exporter is eroded by its random use of economic sanctions. The end of the Cold War shifted the emphasis of the U.S. strategic triad of interests—political, military, and economic—away from the dominance of Cold War politics and military issues, which for 40 years had shunted commercial and trade issues to the side and disadvantaged U.S. economic interests. But the United States still shoots itself in the foot whenever the public is outraged by a television news report. The imposition of unilateral economic sanctions, such as the Cuban Liberty and Democratic Solidarity (Helms-Burton) Act and the Iran, Libya Sanctions Act, have not helped America at all in Asia. The U.S. "hit list" keeps growing, yet people in the United States wonder why their country is not globally competitive. Efforts are under way in Congress to reform sanctions regulations, and the administration is on board many of the proposed constraints. It is time to build credibility with U.S. customers around the world, particularly net food importers in Asia. The United States should not include food and agricultural trade in any unilateral sanction unless there is a state of war.

Participation

The fourth major factor in examining markets is participation, which refers to the ability of individuals to function as consumers in national and global markets. With as much as 75 percent of the population of some developing or emerging Asian markets still living in rural areas, large numbers of consumers remain completely outside the mainstream marketplace.

Prior to the 1997 crisis, economists liked to point out that the Asia-Pacific region was expected to have 1 billion middle class consumers by 2000, including 400 million with purchasing power equal to that of people in the world's wealthiest countries. I believe that this growth will be attained early in the 21st century, although optimism about that potential market base should not override concern about the underlying structural deficiencies in many countries. Observers mesmerized by the current Chinese market should remember that they are looking at the demand of only about 300 million people living in special economic zones or in Beijing or Shanghai. People still live in caves in northeast China, and they still have incomes well below the international poverty line. China's modern development should be viewed as a kind of a westward frontier movement. Spurred by the growth of infrastructure and investment, wealth will increase, pushing development westward, inland from rich coastal areas, and the Chinese market will grow even larger.

Economic recovery in the Asian region will again propel the movement of people from predominantly rural areas to urban centers, which will strain the food system infrastructure in cities and fuel higher food demand. Yet, looking just at urban consumers misses the biggest market potential. In terms of national demographics, the figures are stunning. As noted, the population in Asia's developing economies is about 75 percent rural. From a food standpoint, obviously this is important. Over the next 25 years, an estimated 1.5 billion people in Asia will move from rural areas to developing cities, a staggering statistic considering, as pointed out, that Asia already has a huge number of mega-cities and that these population centers are certainly unsustainable over the long term.

THE CHANGING ASIAN FOOD MARKETPLACE

How will this projected growth affect Asia's food marketplace now and in the long term? Assume that the pre-crisis trends, highlighted next, will resume their upward momentum in the next two years.

First, Asian food processing will again expand because of accelerating levels of FDI and internal capital movement to meet rapidly growing food system demands.

Second, dietary patterns will continue to change as wealth rises. This means an increasing westernization of diet, particularly for the under-15 year olds—the consumers of the future—who are being nurtured on food from McDonald's and other fast-food chains that are becoming common throughout Asia. Dramatically different food consumption patterns are being seen in different demographic sets. Moving toward westernization means consuming more meat and poultry either through exports to the region for conversion to meat in-country or through exports of meat products.

Some Western products need to be tailored to the taste preferences of a diverse Asian market. Products cannot be exported simply as they are. For example, a potato chip may need to be seasoned with spices that are native to the region. In another example, Baskin Robbins had problems selling ice cream cones in South Korea because it was impolite to eat food in the street. So the store had all their employees eat ice cream cones when they went outside, and eating food on the street suddenly became fashionable. Adapting food products and targeting culturally sensitive marketing campaigns are two of the many challenges in dealing with Asian countries. As the Asian economies improve, demand will resurface, money will again grow, and with telecommunications, television, and advertising, there will be abundant opportunities for U.S. agrifood trade.

Third, FDI in the post-crisis Asian markets will further expand the westernization of diets that has taken place over the past two decades by accelerating the growth of Western-style supermarkets and restaurants. These will be stocking a wider variety of food products, providing a market for many well-known U.S. products, specialty food products, and convenience foods. Demand for prepared and convenience foods will also be spurred by the increase of women in the workplace as the economies begin to grow again.

According to this forecast, Asia will apparently be back on the road to the global food market's "nirvana" after a slight detour in 1997-2000. Until the 1997 financial shock, there was good reason to be optimistic about the region's growth potential. Now, however, an important note of caution is in order. Serious potential obstacles to the growth in food trade remain, due not only to a probable rise in protectionist trade policy but also to the region's severe lack of infrastructure. Indeed, existing infrastructure is being eroded in the current economic crisis environment.

THE COMING INFRASTRUCTURE CRISIS

The expansion of U.S. export markets for bulk commodities and particularly for processed food products and consumer food products will be limited over the long term more by infrastructure than by income. One concern is the inadequacy of reliable cold chains—refrigeration and distribution. The United States could have access to much larger consumer markets than it currently has if the appropriate infrastructure existed to move chilled and frozen products to people. In some countries, inadequate power generation can create havoc in trying to move food to consumers. For example, what happens when there is no reliable electricity to maintain the quality of food products? What happens when only a few people know how to handle food products with appropriate modern technology? The lack of adequate refrigeration at ports, rail and truck transport sites, wholesale distribution points, and retail outlets is limiting the ability to safely market many food products. This is true virtually anywhere in the region.

The world community has focused on bringing adequate infrastructure to urban populations. Several Asian cities are larger consumer markets than entire countries in other parts of the world. By 2010, the urban population of East Asia, excluding the developed economies of Japan, South Korea, and Taiwan, will increase from 500 million to 1.2 billion. Further, as discussed, 1.5 billion people will move to cities in Asia over the next 25 years. Urban infrastructure growth to accommodate these vast movements of people will be critical. Tremendous investment in basic infrastructure—water, sewers, roads, bridges, railroads, ports, electricity, and telecommunications—is needed to provide even minimally acceptable urban living conditions.

At the same time, large off-farm investment in rural infrastructure to link crucial agricultural production regions to urban consumers will be required. Without basic infrastructure, rural residents will be forced to migrate to cities to better themselves, and this will add to the environmental and social crisis of unsustainable mega-cities. However, with basic infrastructure investment in rural communities—finance, transportation, telecommunications, electric power, sanitation, education, and health care—agricultural producers will be able to diversify their incomes with off-farm employment, and agricultural processing industries will be able to transform farm production in rural areas and market their products in cities and global markets. Rural residents will have access to improved nutrition through access to markets. U.S. exporters will have a larger consuming public with the financial capacity to purchase higher valued food products.

The United States has a role to play in supporting greater prominence for infrastructure in building the crucial food system linkages. The Export-Import Bank and the Overseas Private Investment Corporation should be encouraged to provide greater support for U.S. business, trade, and investment. The United States must ensure strong support for incorporating projects and product sales related to building modern food systems in the dynamic growth markets in the Pacific Rim, including the macroeconomic investments that are crucial to all sectors. In fact, the United States should make economic infrastructure the top priority at the World Bank and press the Bank to refocus rural development in this direction instead of its traditional emphasis on production agriculture. Although production agriculture is important, the development of the food system and balanced economic growth will be greatly damaged if production agriculture is all that is done. The United States must support policies and programs that build an infrastructure to support all economic activities; then the Pacific Rim food system will be able to take the lead in advancing these countries' economic potential.

CONCLUSION

The U.S. goal of achieving maximum trade opportunities will be possible only if the United States can establish an integrated global food system. The Pacific Rim is a critical linchpin in determining whether this goal will be achieved. However, it would be short-sighted for the United States to focus merely on succeeding in conveying profits to competitive U.S. producers and industries. U.S. agribusinesses that are important players in the Pacific Rim food system have the tremendous responsibility to bring the health, nutrition, food security, and economic benefits of participating in the modern global food system to all people in the region and the world.

2

Assessing the Prospects for Agricultural Trade with Asia

by William T. Coyle

Senior Economist, Asia-Western Hemisphere Branch,
Economic Research Service, U.S. Department of Agriculture

Probably no region of the world is more critical to U.S. agriculture and trade than Asia, despite the Asian financial crisis. This chapter focuses on key themes in U.S. trade with the 15 or so nations that make up East and Southeast Asia. It examines recent projections made by the U.S. Department of Agriculture (USDA) of production, consumption, and trade with China, East Asia, and Southeast Asia, and it discusses public policy issues that have emerged regarding U.S. agricultural trade in the region.

THE CURRENT TRADE SITUATION

East Asia is the most important regional market in the world for U.S. agriculture, even given the downturn from the financial crisis that began in 1997 (Figure 2-1). The United States has had a high and stable share of that market for many years. Japan graduated from the Food for Peace Program (PL 480) in the 1950s, and South Korea graduated from the program in the early 1980s. The U.S. share of the Chinese market is unstable because the United States exports only a few bulk commodities to that market and because China tends to be price sensitive, which results in big fluctuations in trade shares (Figure 2-2). For Southeast Asia, the United States has maintained a share somewhat lower than its share of global agricultural trade, 10-15 percent.

An unmistakable trend in U.S. agricultural trade during the past 10 years has been the shift in the composition of exports from bulk commodities such as grains, oilseeds, and cotton to nonbulk exports, primarily horticultural and livestock products (Figure 2-3). The value of nonbulk commodities exceeded the value of bulk exports to East and Southeast Asia in 1993, 1994, and again in 1997. Overall, the region accounts for almost 40 percent of U.S. exports of nonbulk commodities and more than 70 percent in the case of beef and pork.

The key factors leading to the change in trade composition include economic growth, the weakening U.S. dollar from 1985 to 1995, limits to the increase in livestock production in East Asia, and trade policy break-

FIGURE 2-1
U.S. AGRICULTURAL EXPORTS BY REGION, 1985-98

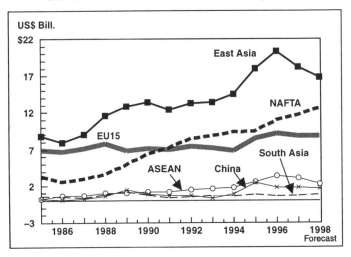

Source: USDA, *Outlook for U.S. Agricultural Exports* (March 1998).

FIGURE 2-2
U.S. SHARE OF AGRICULTURAL TRADE
IN DIFFERENT ASIAN MARKETS, 1962-95

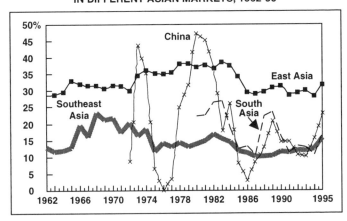

Source: United Nations, COMTRADE database (March 1998).

FIGURE 2-3

U.S. BULK AND NONBULK AGRICULTURAL EXPORTS TO EAST AND
SOUTHEAST ASIA,* 1975-97

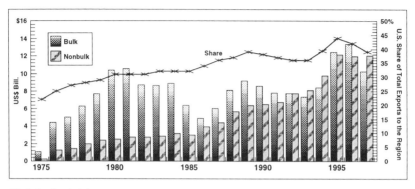

*Excludes South Asia.
Source: FATUS, USDA (March 1998).

throughs. The United States and the countries of East Asia reached bilateral agreements on beef, citrus, and tobacco products in the 1980s. Japan privatized its tobacco monopolies and eased, then eliminated, import quotas on beef, citrus, and other products. South Korea also began to open its beef market in the 1990s. Tedious discussions leading to breakthrough agreements for a few commodities in East Asia have generated billions of dollars in additional U.S. agricultural trade.

PROJECTIONS FOR PRODUCTION, CONSUMPTION, AND TRADE

The focus on China in the past few years is the result of that country's incredible swing in grain trade. In the early 1990s, China was second to the United States as a net exporter of grain. Within one year, it became a net importer, a swing of more than 20 million metric tons, or about 10 percent of global grain trade. This shift drew considerable attention, including publication in 1995 of Lester Brown's book, *Who Will Feed China? Wake Up Call for a Small Planet.*[1] Brown envisioned China as following a path similar to East Asia's, with urbanization encroaching on agricultural land, grain production slowly declining, and income-driven meat consumption rising, leading to a huge gap between consumption and production of grain by 2030. He predicted a grain import number that was unbelievable.

But China's grain production in 1996-98 reached record levels. As a consequence, China imported only 5 million metric tons of grain in 1996, 4 million in 1997, and 5 million in 1998, compared with 16 million metric tons in 1995. China has returned to being a small net exporter of grain, as it was in 1992-93. U.S. agricultural exports to China have declined from $1.8 billion in FY1997 to $1.5 billion in FY1998. China remains a fairly small market. These events are a reminder that one or two years do not necessarily constitute a trend.

⌒ Southeast Asia is a significant market in the sense that it grew rapidly from 1993 to 1996. U.S. exports to the region more than doubled during that period, surpassing $3.2 billion in 1996. Since then, exports have dropped, in part due to the financial crisis.

Key factors that will affect this region's future are the same that affected its recent past:

- *Economic growth.* Forecasters project that, once the financial crisis has passed, economic growth in East and Southeast Asia will be above the world average. Consequently, the shift in the global economy's center of gravity toward this part of the world will resume after the financial crisis has played out.

- *Growth of Asia's middle class.* The Economist predicted an increase of one billion middle class consumers in Asia by 2000, and DRI/McGraw Hill projected that middle class households in China would rise from 35 million in 1997 to about 150 million in 2010.

- *Dietary change.* Because economic growth drives dietary changes, diets in East Asia, Southeast Asia, and China are becoming more resource-intensive and meat-oriented.

- *Comparative advantage.* The abundant resource in this part of the world is not land, but labor, both unskilled and skilled.

- *Policy reform.* Although the implementation of the Uruguay Round of the General Agreement on Tariffs and Trade resulted in more transparency and a framework for the future, there is still much unfinished business. In addition to a World Trade Organization round in 1999, the initiative of the Asia-Pacific Economic Cooperation forum is seeking freer trade by 2010 for developed country members and by 2020 for developing country members. If successful, these efforts will produce substantial gains in food and agricultural trade because protection, particularly in East Asia, remains significant in these sectors.

The Economic Research Service (ERS) of the USDA annually projects worldwide production, consumption, and trade of major commodities. According to ERS, despite the short-term financial shock, East and Southeast Asia will lead the regions in the world in the growth of grain imports over the next 10 years (Figure 2-4). ERS projects that China and the Association of Southeast Asian Nations (ASEAN) will be important growth markets for grain imports. East Asia will still import large quantities of coarse grain, but growth will slow. East Asia will increasingly substitute imports of meat for imports of grain (Figure 2-5).

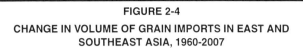

FIGURE 2-4

CHANGE IN VOLUME OF GRAIN IMPORTS IN EAST AND
SOUTHEAST ASIA, 1960-2007

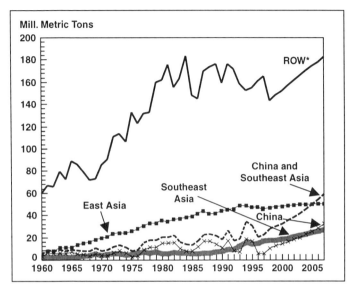

*ROW = rest of world.
Source: ERS, USDA, International Agricultural Baseline Projections to 2007 (August 1998).

As China's economy expands and incomes rise, meat consumption will increase, but will likely remain well below per capita levels in North America. Grain production will grow more slowly than consumption, but rapidly enough to keep self-sufficiency well above 90 percent, probably the lowest level that China's leaders would allow. As diets change, consumption of coarse grain and wheat will rise, and rice consumption will decline. Greater application of higher yielding seeds, better management, and increased use of other inputs, especially in China's interior, are expected to boost China's grain output as grain area declines. Output could also rise if farmers double-crop a larger area in the southern provinces. China's yields have ample leeway to rise in the future. Yields are lower than currently reported in official statistics because the size of the planted area has been significantly underestimated.

After the financial crisis wanes, a similar gap between grain consumption and production is expected to develop in the ASEAN-4 (Indonesia, Malaysia, the Philippines, and Thailand) in the next decade. In contrast with China, ASEAN has virtually no wheat production because of the countries' tropical climate, although per capita wheat consumption is generally ex-

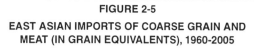

FIGURE 2-5

EAST ASIAN IMPORTS OF COARSE GRAIN AND
MEAT (IN GRAIN EQUIVALENTS), 1960-2005

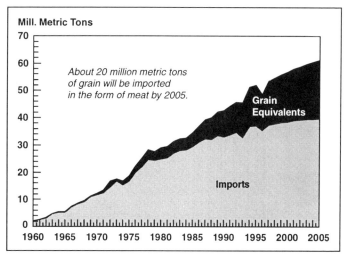

Source: See Figure 2-4.

panding. Also in contrast with China, rice production in ASEAN is projected to increase on the strength of expanding planted area and rising yields. Led by Thailand and Vietnam, ASEAN is expected to become more prominent as a rice-exporting region in the future. In the short term, Indonesia will be importing larger-than-normal volumes of rice because of drought and fires related to El Niño weather patterns.

Short-term economic prospects in ASEAN are uncertain because of the financial crisis. But once the crisis passes, the larger economies are expected to grow by at least 4 to 5 percent annually in the 2000-05 period. Import demand for wheat and coarse grain will increase to support expanding domestic wheat flour and livestock industries. Thailand, for example, was an important exporter of corn through the mid-1980s, but it is now a slight net importer as domestic producers of poultry and pork have stepped up production to meet domestic and export demand. After declining in the short term, poultry production will rise in the intermediate term, 2000-05, stimulating even greater grain demand. However, Thai poultry exports are forecast to stabilize as a larger share of production is sold locally. In East Asia, an enormous gap between consumption and production has existed for some time (Figure 2-6). Coarse grain consumption will level off because of rising costs in expanding domestic meat production and increased meat import competition.

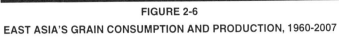

FIGURE 2-6

EAST ASIA'S GRAIN CONSUMPTION AND PRODUCTION, 1960-2007

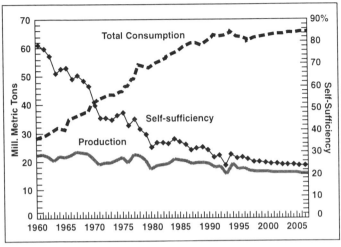

Source: See Figure 2-4.

In sum, the outlook is favorable for East and Southeast Asian imports of bulk commodities such as grain, oilseeds, and cotton once the region has worked its way out of its current economic difficulties. Furthermore, increased meat imports in East Asia are likely over the next decade, and continued increases for other processed products are expected in the intermediate term (2000-05).

EMERGING PUBLIC POLICY ISSUES

U.S. policy toward East and Southeast Asia should have three dimensions. First, the importance of economic growth cannot be underestimated, as recent events clearly demonstrate. Economic growth drives many changes including expansion of trade; thus, the United States should support policies that enhance growth, or recovery, in these markets.

The next important dimension is access to markets where outstanding issues, particularly in East Asia, need to be addressed, such as high tariffs on beef and citrus in Japan and on ice cream and chilled pork in South Korea. The flow of investment should be facilitated. For many multinational companies, their subsidiary sales in foreign countries are much more important than their exports of processed products to those markets. Trade in capital and technology associated with food manufacturing, for example, is much larger than trade in manufactured foods. Technical barriers such as sanitary and phytosanitary issues also impede market access. In terms of the value of the affected trade, about 50 percent of the problems are in East Asia, particularly China, Japan, and South Korea. Finally, infrastructure bottlenecks need to be reduced in developing countries. It is no surprise that about three-fourths of U.S. exports of consumer-ready and processed products go to middle and high income countries. Expansion of this trade in other markets such as China and Southeast Asia will depend not only on demand-side factors but also on critical supply-side factors, including port capacity, refrigeration capacity, air shipping capacity, and marketing know-how.

NOTE

1. Lester Brown, *Who Will Feed China? Wake Up Call for a Small Planet* (New York: Norton, 1995).

PART II

THE POTENTIAL FOR GROWTH IN TRADE AND INVESTMENT— A POLICY PERSPECTIVE

3

Shifts in World Agricultural Trade

by Sherman Robinson

Director, Trade and Macroeconomics Division, International Food Policy Research Institute

From a trade policy perspective, two major trends, especially in Asia, will determine the direction of the world economy during the next 25 years. First is the postwar trend of global liberalization, to which the United States has given continuing support from one round of the General Agreement on Tariffs and Trade (GATT) to the next, in a more or less steady progression, through the Uruguay Round. Second, regional trading agreements have proliferated. Major blocs now in place include the North Atlantic Free Trade Agreement (NAFTA) and the Southern Cone Common Market (MERCOSUR, its Spanish acronym). Numerous others are being formed or are under discussion in Latin America, Africa, and Asia. In Asia, the countries constituting the Asia-Pacific Economic Cooperation (APEC) forum have agreed to negotiate to form a free trade area, and the Association of Southeast Asian Nations (ASEAN) has discussed establishing a separate free trade area. Although the financial crisis in Asia beginning in 1997 has focused attention on capital markets and macroeconomic stability, all these countries recognize the need to expand trade as they emerge from the crisis, and renewed policy interest in regional trading arrangements can be expected.

The proliferation of regional trading blocks raises concerns about sustaining progress toward global liberalization under the World Trade Organization. New WTO negotiations are supposed to begin in 1999 with a focus on agriculture, which continues to be a difficult area for agreement. Partially spurred by the Uruguay Round, domestic policy reforms in agriculture are under way in many developed and less developed countries, but there are doubts about the depth of commitment to these reforms.

GLOBAL TRENDS

Despite these uncertainties, four major trends are likely to prevail over the next two decades or so.

- First, given that the Uruguay Round has been successfully completed, the prospects for continued liberalization of global trade, including agriculture, are bright. Also, continued liberalization in domestic agricultural policies can be expected, though with some difficulties along the way.

- Second, agricultural trade will become more important, especially for developing countries. For these countries, the often-stated goal of achieving self-sufficiency in food production is neither practical nor desirable.

- Third, more regional trading agreements will emerge and evolve.

- Finally, for developing countries, trade liberalization is probably less important in promoting growth and well-being than is domestic policy reform. Trade reform and domestic policy reform tend to go together, but there are tensions that must be confronted politically to maintain a balance.

Projections for Key Areas

At the International Food Policy Research Institute (IFPRI), projections of world agricultural production and trade over the next 20 to 25 years are largely driven by assumptions in three key areas. First, will all the Organization for Economic Cooperation and Development (OECD) countries—the developed countries—be successful in the agricultural policy reforms on which they have embarked? Progress so far is encouraging, but much has been left for the future. Will the OECD countries continue the reform process and also support continued agricultural trade and domestic liberalization in the next round of WTO negotiations?

Second, major changes are occurring in the former socialist countries of eastern Europe and the Soviet Union. Early in the 20th century, many of these countries were major agricultural producers and exporters. Will they resume their historical role in the world economy? Their relations with the European Union (EU), in particular, are crucial.

Third, any projections regarding world agriculture depend strongly on what happens to the composition of income in developing countries. Middle and upper income households have very different consumption patterns than poor households, just as consumption patterns between urban and rural households differ. Income growth and urbanization are important.

Over a period of 25 years, what happens in rural-urban migration will have an enormous impact on the structure of demand for agriculture.

In the early 1990s, the OECD countries dominated the world economy, and they still dominate world trade. But a number of developing countries are beginning to become important because they are growing (the semi-industrial countries), are large (e.g., India, Bangladesh, Brazil, and Indonesia), or are both (e.g., China). While intra-OECD trade still greatly exceeds trade between the OECD countries and the rest of the world, "north-south" trade will increase in the future. Trade is important for the East Asian newly industrialized countries (NICs) and for the big Asian economies such as India, Bangladesh, and China. These nations have become much more trade dependent, a trend that will continue.

Looking at the sectoral structure of gross domestic product (GDP), agricultural shares are quite high in the poor countries. Agriculture is still an enormous sector in sub-Saharan Africa, representing 36 percent of GDP, on average. In South Asia and China, the agricultural share is 30 percent, and in Latin America, it averages 10 percent. The NICs are somewhat lower, with agriculture around 8 percent. However, in the OECD countries, agriculture is around 2.5 percent of GDP. Thus, for poor countries, agriculture has an overwhelmingly important economic role as well as a significant role in their international trade. This pattern will continue far into the next century, even though the share of agriculture in their economies is projected to decline as these countries grow.

Growth in World Population, Income, and Urbanization

These agricultural trends are at work in an environment of a rapidly growing world population, with high rates of growth in Africa and Asia (with Asia starting from a higher base). Sometime in the middle of the next century, when the world reaches a steady-state population, most people will be Asian. In addition, by 2020, the majority of the population worldwide will be urban. Asian cities will be extremely large, and infrastructure investment will be critical to serve them. The aggregate consumption pattern will differ greatly from today's because urban populations buy more processed foods. Based on projections of aggregate income and population growth, food demand in developing countries will increase rapidly. Concomitant with income growth and urbanization will be significant growth in the demand for meats.

Cereal production in developing countries will increase, based on extrapolations from past trends in productivity growth. Yet, there is unease about such optimistic projections. In the postwar period, several agricultural revolutions have occurred—mechanization, chemical, and biological (new seeds). The next revolution may be genetic manipulation. Clearly, there is scope in the developing world for increased productivity growth through wider dissemination of existing technologies. Even so, there is a worrisome undertone at meetings of the international agricultural research centers about whether productivity increases will continue at past rates. Continuation of past technology growth worldwide will certainly not occur without serious investment in research. Now is not the time to cut investment in agricultural research.

☞ World agricultural trade will also significantly increase as a share of world supply and demand. Countries gain from specialization, and potential exporters such as the United States have an enormous interest in making the world safe for world trade so that countries can pursue comparative advantage. The OECD countries as a group are projected to increase agricultural exports to the rest of the world, especially to markets in Asia and, to a lesser extent, Africa.

However, projections of grain trade are sensitive to projections of changes in food demand, especially meats. Meat demand is sensitive to urbanization and income growth by demand groups—income distribution matters as much as aggregate income growth. Varying assumptions about the distribution of income produce a wide range of answers about meat demand and therefore an even greater variation in projections of grain demand. While these projections seem reasonable, there is a large margin for error. Nevertheless, the basic projection of an increased role for grain trade seems secure, despite wide variations in assumptions about other trends.

THE POLICY ENVIRONMENT

Trade reform is an important part of total agricultural policy reform around the world. The links between international trade reform and domestic policy reform in agriculture were certainly at the center of the Uruguay Round negotiations. Many believe, correctly, that there would not have been as much policy reform in the United States and Europe as has occurred if the Uruguay Round had been unsuccessful. Further progress will depend on a continued balancing of agricultural reform in the domestic and international trade arenas.

Both the United States and the EU, however, have ducked many issues. The test will come when the next round of WTO negotiations begins in 2000 and when world markets may well be weaker than they are now. Then there will be real tension.

Assuring an Open, Stable Trading Regime

International institutions such as the World Bank are suggesting to developing countries that agricultural trade will become increasingly important for them and thus they should not seek food self-sufficiency. Instead, they should depend on a liberal, open world trading system to provide a reliable supply of food when needed. If this view is to prevail, the developed countries must behave responsibly. In response to a rise in world agricultural prices a few years ago, the EU limited exports to protect its domestic consumers. When world prices fell, the EU subsidized exports. Such behavior tends to destabilize world markets and raises reasonable concerns in developing countries.

It also does not help that the United States sometimes acts like a bully. In 1993, the United States accused Canada of being an evil subsidizer of wheat exports. It then used the Export Enhancement Program (EEP) to subsidize U.S. wheat exports to the Mexican market, right at the end of the NAFTA negotiations. Mexico was in the process of reforming its domestic agricultural programs and did not welcome subsidized sales into its markets. Such behavior by the United States is hardly a good neighbor policy. Under NAFTA, whose goal is to integrate markets across North America, substantial work is needed to coordinate agricultural policies.

To achieve gains from specialization, countries must operate in a world environment where self-sufficiency is unnecessary because they can rely on trade in a stable world market. Countries then will not need to produce and store massive buffer stocks of grains, an expensive undertaking.

One intriguing trend reflecting potential gains from specialization is the significant growth in many countries in production of specialty crops such as fruits, flowers, and vegetables. For example, in Indonesia, major investments in roads and other infrastructure around Jakarta have provided farmers who are growing horticultural crops easier access to Jakarta's urban markets. Rather than growing grains on high value irrigated land, developing countries should develop a comparative advantage in high value, labor-intensive specialty crops. However, to exploit this comparative advantage, these countries must pursue major investments in infrastructure, including roads and communications, which require government involvement. Further, the developed countries must open their markets.

There has been a lengthy debate on the links between trade and wages. The United States worries that opening up trade will lower the wages of U.S. unskilled labor—the "race to the bottom." As evidenced by the GATT and the NAFTA debates, the fear is real and widespread among workers, especially unionized workers. Although the debate is active and globalization of production is having profound effects on specialization across countries, the major problem for workers is not increased trade; rather, as former U.S. Secretary of Labor Robert B. Reich has argued, it is skill upgrading. Changes in technology and in the skill structure of the labor force have far more important effects on wages than changes in commodity trade flows.

REGIONAL AND GLOBAL INTEGRATION

Trade theory holds that regional trading agreements may have negative results. If their sole accomplishment is to divert trade from low cost producers outside the bloc to high cost producers within the bloc, such agreements increase costs to consumers and should not be pursued. Trade theorists have also expressed concern that the focus on regional trading blocs shifts policy attention away from seeking further global trade reform. Although some argued that the creation of NAFTA would make it more difficult to complete the Uruguay Round negotiations, this was not the case.

The fundamental question regarding regional trading agreements is whether they create more trade than they divert. There is now a history of experience with some of these agreements and considerable empirical work exploring their potential effects. Overall, while some evidence of trade diversion can be found, the empirical finding is that, in virtually every regional trading bloc that has been analyzed, trade creation is much larger than trade diversion. On balance, trade blocs appear to be good—"welfare increasing," in the jargon. This view is certainly consistent with historical experience. The European common market was enormously trade-creating, and early experience with NAFTA and MERCOSUR indicates that the projections of large trade creation that emerged from modeling work are correct.

The Benefits of Both

However, analysis indicates a caveat to the general proposition that regional trading blocs are good: To be effective, a free trade agreement should include at least one large, preferably rich, partner. For example, an ASEAN free trade area that included only the poorer countries in the region or a Central American free trade agreement that excluded Mexico and the United States would probably have little success.

In a study of the potential gains from forming an APEC free trade area, IFPRI considered the effects of excluding a large nation (say, the United States). The results indicate that it is not in the interest of the member countries to exclude any big partner. The excluded country loses, but the countries in the smaller bloc are also worse off than they would be in a larger bloc. This is an intriguing empirical result because it implies a strong economic argument for being as inclusive as possible in negotiating an APEC free trade agreement. This result generalizes in that it is worthwhile to add other countries to the free trade area—global liberalization is potentially better for everyone. In other words, regional trade agreements benefit their members, but globalization benefits them even more.

Thus, regional trading agreements do not detract from the desirability of seeking further global liberalization under the WTO; there is no necessary inconsistency between the two. Continued global liberalization is important to pursue, and forming and expanding regional free trade areas are useful steps along the way. Regional agreements also tend to be easier to negotiate than a global agreement.

CONCLUSIONS

From the perspective of developing countries, the fall of communism leaves only the free market paradigm; the socialist model is no longer seen as a viable alternative. This paradigm provides a guide to policy formulation, relying on competition, capitalism, open markets, and low protection levels in an environment of macroeconomic stability. Many former socialist countries in eastern Europe and the developing world have undergone major structural adjustment programs designed to achieve macroeconomic stability and to launch a new development strategy. With the successful completion of the Uruguay Round, the OECD countries have also made a good start at agricultural policy reform—albeit with much hesitation, nationalistic rhetoric, and some backsliding.

Since World War II, and especially since the Korean War, the growth of world trade has been amazing, far outstripping the growth in world GDP. Trade shares have increased in almost all countries of the world. The global economy is expanding, with increasing specialization and interdependence in production. Agricultural trade has also increased, but not as fast as trade in industrial products. Over the next 25 years, agricultural trade is projected to expand greatly, providing opportunities for gains from specialization, as many countries exploit their comparative advantage. If these gains are to spread to the developing world, it must be assured an open and stable trading system. Developing countries have long viewed food grains as strategic commodities, requiring government support to avoid the danger of politically destabilizing price rises or, worse, shortages due to the actions of other countries. The Uruguay Round initiated a process of trade reform and concomitant domestic policy reform in many countries. To pursue policies that take advantage of these trends, the developing countries must be convinced that the developed countries will remain committed to the reform process. This commitment will be tested in the next round of negotiations under the WTO.

The reform process will likely continue—the momentum exists and the potential gains are real and widely perceived. But there are also real dangers of setbacks. The inability of the U.S. Congress to grant the President fast track negotiating authority is a bad sign, as is the EU's apparent difficulty in continuing reform of its Common Agricultural Policy and in opening up to eastern Europe. It would certainly be advantageous for the developing countries to organize themselves in preparation for the next round of trade negotiations. They have common interests in seeing the process of agricultural reform continue in the developed countries and in gaining access to these markets for their own agricultural products.

4

Changes in the Structure of Agricultural Trade with Asia in the 1990s

by John Dyck

*Team Leader, Asia-Western Hemisphere Branch,
Economic Research Service, U.S. Department of Agriculture*

U.S. agricultural trade with Asia is immense, relatively stable, and generally growing. Trade is mainly one way, with the United States exporting a large amount and importing relatively little (see Figure 4-1 for the growth of U.S. agricultural exports to Asia). Exports to East Asia, including China, and Southeast Asia, account for about 40 percent of total U.S. agricultural exports and are in sharp contrast to the volatile, often declining exports to other major regions such as the European Union (EU) and the former Soviet Union. However, there has also been volatility in the Asian markets in the 1990s. This chapter reviews the decade's trade record and examines the structural shifts that have occurred in U.S. agricultural exports.

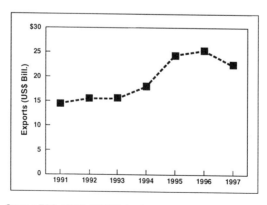

FIGURE 4-1

**U.S. AGRICULTURAL EXPORTS TO EAST AND
SOUTHEAST ASIA, 1991-97**

Source: ERS, USDA, DARTS database.

THE TRADE RECORD OF THE 1990s

U.S. agricultural trade with Asia increased considerably during the 1990s, continuing a history of growth that began in the 1950s. In fact, growth in U.S. agricultural trade with Asia was so predictable that it was sometimes taken for granted. However, the financial crisis that exploded in 1997 demonstrated that this trade was not simple, but complex, and that parts of it were fragile.

The growing complexity of Asian trade was an exciting phenomenon before the crisis occurred. The agricultural goods imported by Asian markets were becoming much more diverse, as were the suppliers of those goods to Asia. In this changing environment, U.S. agricultural exporters found both challenges and opportunities.

The years 1994 and 1995 were heady for U.S. agricultural exports to Asia, and they stand out in the trade record. The value of U.S. exports jumped by $8.9 billion during the course of those two years (Figure 4-2). Total exports in 1995 were 57 percent larger than in 1993. The reasons for the increase illustrate important trends.

In the 1960s and 1970s, U.S. grain exports to Asia grew substantially, sharing the market with grain exports from Australia and Canada. After the mid-1980s, new competitors emerged: the EU, eastern Europe, and especially China, all of whom took major parts of the grain market away from the United States. In 1994-95, China suddenly ceased its grain exports and began to import corn. Chinese oilseed and cotton exports also declined. It became evident that China's own demand for feed was rising so rapidly that the country would henceforth have to be concerned more with deficits than

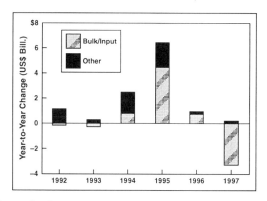

FIGURE 4-2

ANNUAL CHANGES IN U.S. AGRICULTURAL EXPORTS TO EAST AND SOUTHEAST ASIA, 1992-97

Source: See Figure 4-1.

surpluses. China could no longer be regarded as a long-term net exporter of corn. China's market share of corn, particularly large in South Korea, was almost entirely regained by U.S. exporters. Strong commodity prices in 1994-95 also boosted the value of U.S. agricultural exports. The switch in China's trade flows and the severe drought in Australia tightened grain supplies worldwide, and the United States shipped larger volumes at higher prices to Asia. In 1994-95, U.S. exports of grain and other bulk commodities (oilseeds and cotton) rose by $2 billion to South Korea and Japan, by $500 million to Southeast Asia, and by $1.9 billion to China.

Growth in Consumer-Ready Goods

Another, largely unrelated, development also helped to increase U.S. trade in 1994 and 1995. While the effect of the Chinese about-face was felt in bulk commodities, there was a $2.5 billion increase in consumer-ready goods (Figure 4-3). Japan, the largest agricultural import market in the world, led the way. The yen strengthened to unprecedented levels (Figure 4-4), weather was turbulent, trade barriers were being lowered, and imports surged. The increase in consumer-ready goods shattered Japan's image of stability and slow growth in agricultural imports and left agricultural exporters to Japan delighted and curious. More generally, it provided evidence of the kind of trade growth that may occur elsewhere as economies reach maturity at high levels of wealth. Consumer-ready goods include meats, fruits, vegetables, processed foods, beverages, and others. Although meats are the leading category by value, consumer-ready products are diverse, and many of them were scarcely traded to Asian countries only a decade ago.

FIGURE 4-3

U.S. AGRICULTURAL EXPORTS TO EAST AND SOUTHEAST ASIA, BY CATEGORY, 1990-97

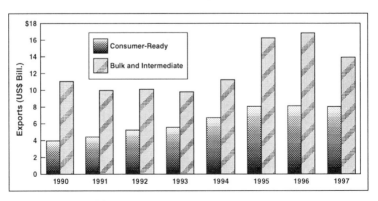

Source: FAS, USDA, BICO database.

FIGURE 4-4

YEN PER DOLLAR
NOMINAL EXCHANGE RATE, 1987-97
(Annual Averages)

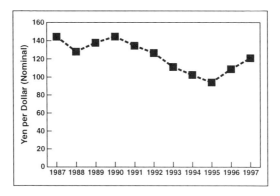

Source: IMF, *International Financial Statistics.*

Market analysts speak of a retail food revolution that took place in Japan in the early to mid-1990s. The revolution occurred within an outwardly stagnant Japanese economy that showed little growth after the speculative "bubble" economy burst in 1989. The economic stagnation ended income growth for many households and frightened consumers, resulting, according to Japanese retailers, in more price-conscious behavior. Supermarkets competed to lower prices, and sourcing supplies overseas permitted strong price reductions, especially given the high level of the yen. Supermarkets and associated convenience stores and hypermarkets (very large consumer-goods retail outlets) also sought to lower marketing costs between farm production and retail display by reducing the complexity of the distribution system and the number of wholesale transactions involved. Direct contracts with farmers both inside and outside Japan and longer-term buying arrangements with wholesalers and importers that specified quality, price, and timing increasingly replaced reliance on wholesale market auctions. Supermarkets expanded both in size per store and in number of stores; small food shops went out of business. Overall, the number of retail food outlets decreased, while their average size increased, partly because of changes in Japan's laws on retail store size. This decrease in outlets also helped to simplify the marketing chain and to cut costs. U.S. exports of supermarket-ready agricultural goods to Japan rose by $1.5 billion during 1994-95.

Agricultural imports in the consumer-ready categories rose in other markets, too. Hong Kong has long been an excellent import market for foods. However, in the 1990s, China, especially the prosperous area around Hong Kong, also showed a taste for U.S. products such as chicken paws (feet), red meats, beverages, vegetables, and snack foods. China's imports from the United States, including those of Hong Kong, rose by $425 million. Taiwan's imports rose by $110 million in the consumer-ready category, while Southeast Asian imports rose by $105 in the two years. In both Taiwan and Southeast Asia, fresh fruits led the trade growth. Finally, the loosening of South Korea's trade protections led to a $300 million increase in U.S. exports of beef, processed fruits and vegetables, and oranges.

In 1996, U.S. exports grew only slightly, and trade to China fell. Then, in 1997, trade to all of Asia declined, and in 1998, the decline became steeper. The yen began to weaken in 1996 and dropped significantly in 1997, making Japan's imports from the United States more expensive. China resumed its corn exports on a limited scale in 1997. World bulk commodity prices decreased, and the value of bulk exports to most Asian countries fell in 1997 and 1998. However, consumer-ready trade held its own in 1997. In late 1997, the effects of the financial crisis began to be noticeable in U.S. agricultural trade. Southeast Asian and Korean currencies lost value, Indonesia turned to exporting corn when livestock feeding there plummeted, and companies in several countries experienced difficulty in paying for imports. Trade data for the first eight months of 1998 show that consumer-ready exports to Asia fell, but by less than did bulk exports.

In some respects, the current trade experience resembles a roller-coaster ride. But the rather dramatic events related to agricultural trade in the 1990s have given important evidence about Asia's food and fiber markets that requires some adjustment of popular thinking about the nature and growth of these markets.

THE CHANGING NATURE OF ASIA'S FOOD AND FIBER MARKETS

In Asia in the 1970s, imports were predominantly inputs for further production. Examples include cotton, hides, rubber, and other raw materials for industry and feed grains and oilseeds for animal production. These inputs were used to produce goods for domestic consumption, especially meat and animal products, and to produce Asia's important textile and footwear exports. They were often imported rather freely with low tariffs. Agricultural imports for more direct use were limited and faced high tariffs, quotas, or total bans. For commodities that the importing countries deemed sensitive, state trading was common.

Given this trade environment, U.S. agriculture had to pin its hopes on rising incomes in the Asian countries, which would lead to greater consumption of meats, eggs, dairy products, and wheat products and thus to greater imports of the underlying inputs. While the prices of the input commodities exported by the United States had to be competitive with other exporters' prices, the number of other exporters of bulk commodities was often limited, and domestic production in the importing countries was usually negligible.

In the 1980s, some markets, primarily Japan, began to buy a broader array of agricultural exports from the United States. Rather than providing the input, feed, U.S. exporters increasingly sold the output, meat. Japanese markets were penetrated by other value-added products such as orange juice, frozen and canned fruits and vegetables, and highly processed foods and food mixes. Significant amounts of high value fresh and dried produce, such as fresh fruits, nuts, dried beans, and dried fruit, were also imported by Japan and, to a lesser extent, by Hong Kong and Taiwan.

This trend accelerated in the 1990s. The lowering of trade barriers and increasingly sophisticated transportation and marketing created many new markets for agricultural trade first in Japan and Hong Kong, but increasingly in the countries of Southeast Asia and in Taiwan, South Korea, and China.

The new trade differs in several respects from the earlier bulk trade. In most cases, the product being imported is also produced domestically in the importing country. The imported product must compete against the domestic product on quality and price. Seasonality and weather are important because they affect not just the exporting country's supply but also the importing country's supply. Bulk exports are often imported by a limited number of firms, and end users of those firms' products (e.g., shirts or domestically produced meats) may have little idea of the origin of the inputs. However, consumer-ready imports are often identified by country of origin to the final consumers, who number in the millions. Advertising and food safety assurance are critical but complicated operations. Japan and Hong Kong have been the laboratories in which this trade has been explored, and the widening of the trade to other markets in Asia has often occurred as an offshoot of original marketing in Japan and Hong Kong, where consumer-ready trade now rivals bulk trade in size.

Trade in consumer-ready products is often part of a choice that a firm can make. The firm can ship a finished product to a foreign market, or it can ship inputs to the foreign market and process or package them there through a subsidiary it has established or through a partner firm. Labor for processing is available in all Asian markets, at various wage rates, and processing near the point of consumption can have tariff and tax advantages, as well as being an efficient way to obtain the information needed to tailor the product to a particular market. In practice, many Asian markets are hard to penetrate without a local partner. All these factors have stimulated a large investment in food processing in Asia by U.S. firms and multinational operations that rely on U.S. raw materials. Growing wealth and the increasing desire for U.S. foods in Asian countries will further stimulate U.S. firms to invest in processing in those countries as well as to ship consumer-ready processed foods directly to them. Even in the former case, however, many of the food ingredients are likely to be imported from the United States.

THE NEED TO RETHINK ASIA'S PROSPECTS

Characterizing a market as mature is fraught with peril. Japan was often relegated to the mature category before 1994, when its agricultural imports surged, as noted above. Deregulation and trade liberalization, as well as the consolidation of the retail food industry in Japan, are likely to continue to change the Japanese market and increase the volume of consumer-ready imports and the inputs needed for food processing in Japan.

Similarly, other assumptions or stereotypes about Asian markets can be relied on too heavily. Several such areas are explored below.

Reevaluating Asian Agricultural Protectionist Policies

The Uruguay Round of the General Agreement on Tariffs and Trade put agricultural goods firmly under the discipline of the World Trade Organization (WTO). Regional agreements such as the Asia-Pacific Economic Cooperation (APEC) forum have ambitious targets for liberalizing all trade. However, the strength of protectionist thought and actions in Asia should not be underestimated, and continual progress toward free trade should not be taken for granted. Japan and South Korea have been willing to incur high costs to protect their rice markets since the ratification of the Uruguay Round in 1994. Japan's government has bought substantial amounts of high quality rice in several foreign markets, only to let it languish in expensive, refrigerated warehouses where its palatability to Japanese consumers is reduced after a year or two. Although some of the rice has been used as animal feed or donated as food aid, neither use has recouped the government's purchase cost. South Korea has satisfied its minimum access commitment by purchasing rice that is of low value to Korean consumers. The pro forma buying dashed the hopes of foreign rice producers that the Uruguay Round had provided a true opening to the South Korean market.

China and some Southeast Asian countries have looked with interest on the model of agricultural development that Northeast Asia (Japan, South Korea, and Taiwan) pursued in the 1970s: Maximize self-sufficiency in foods and treat agricultural imports as a burden rather than an opportunity in many cases. The negotiations for the entry of China into the WTO and the economic distress experienced in Southeast Asia in 1997-98 may prompt reevaluation of future agricultural protectionism, which leads to high cost foods and inefficient farm production.

The protectionism of the past in Northeast Asia has left a legacy of small farms (the average area owned by a farm household is about one hectare) and a large number of aging farmers. When trade liberalization opens these markets, domestic production often falls. Within Northeast Asia and elsewhere, the assumption is widespread that production will continually slide. This can be misleading. With the right investment and management, a farm in Northeast Asia can do much with a small area. Asia has large numbers of vinyl and glass greenhouses, and they support vigorous, high yield production of high quality vegetables and fruits. Also, farms in Northeast Asia are not inevitably small. While it is still expensive to buy farmland (although costs have dropped in the past decade), farm expansion can take place by grouping small holdings under the management of one farm, firm, or cooperative, which operates them like a large farm, without ownership changing hands. It is unwise to project a collapse or a steady contraction in production even for Northeast Asia, and production in the rest of Asia may become more competitive with imports at an earlier stage than in Japan. Asian producers have formidable advantages in commodities like rice, where the natural endowment is favorable, and in fruits, vegetables, and livestock products, where a premium is attached to freshness.

Exploring Complementarities Between the United States and Asia

Analysis of U.S. agricultural competitiveness includes the relative costs of farm production around the world. However, trade with Asia demonstrates that this is not the only factor shaping trade flows. The rising volume of consumer-ready product trade is also strongly influenced by the costs of processing and transportation and by differences in preferences among countries. For some commodities, trade is very specific or differentiated. The United States can ship chicken legs to Japan, but not breast meat because its wholesale price is lower in Japan than in the United States, even though the cost of producing broilers is higher in Japan. Japanese consumers do not favor breast meat, while U.S. consumers do. The price of breast meat is bid up in the United States, but discounted in Japan. The large U.S. export trade in meat offal and chicken parts also depends less on cheaper animal production in the United States than on differing consumer demand on the two sides of the Pacific. The preference for chicken paws is very low in the United States, but strong in China. Both Chinese consumers and U.S. producers gain from this trade. More such complementarities will continue to emerge as firms in the United States and Asia explore their opportunities.

Misestimating the Cost of Asian Labor

The cost of labor in Asian farming and food-processing deserves more study. The assumption is often made that, aside from Northeast Asia, Hong Kong, and Singapore, labor is quite cheap because of widespread underemployment. The region is assigned major competitive advantages in labor-intensive fruit and vegetable production and as a site for food-processing plants. The actual record is not so clear. Because its domestic farm labor was too expensive, Thailand was importing labor from Burma until the recent economic crisis, and Malaysia was importing labor from Indonesia. There were reports of changes in Chinese farming practices as labor migrated out of agriculture. Food-processing plants are often located near other industries and around major cities where labor is relatively more expensive. While Southeast Asia's wages relative to the rest of the world have now fallen, and foreign investment in China continues in order to tap cheaper labor there, it is unwise to overestimate how cheap Asian labor is and how decisive labor costs alone are in determining the location of specialty farming and food processing.

In the 1980s, the rise of labor costs in Northeast Asia forced garment making and shoe manufacturing out of that region, and light manufacturing shifted heavily to China and Southeast Asia. The shift was profound and relatively rapid, and there were expectations that U.S. cotton and hide exports would shift away from Northeast Asia as well. However, the decline in U.S. fiber exports to Northeast Asia has been gradual. It is now clear that spinning and tanning are firmly rooted in Northeast Asia. Yarn and leather from these operations are being sent to other parts of Asia to be made into finished products. The basic processing is capital intensive, so that textile and shoe firms are slow to give up expensive plants in Northeast Asia and construct new ones elsewhere. As garment and shoe assembly follow lower labor costs, the growth of these industries in China and most of Southeast Asia appears to be faltering, and countries with even lower labor costs, such as Bangladesh, Sri Lanka, Cambodia, North Korea, and those outside Asia, show growing output. Given the volatility in the location of textile and shoe manufacture, the flow of cotton and hides for processing may remain directed to Northeast Asia for some time.

INFLUENCES ON U.S. AGRICULTURAL EXPORTS IN THE NEXT DECADE

Trade liberalization will continue to boost the value and increase the diversity of U.S. agricultural exports. The admission of China and Taiwan to the WTO will result in lower barriers against U.S. exports. The Uruguay Round liberalizations will continue in Japan through 2000 and in other Asian signatories through 2004. Monopolies and oligopolies whose existence depends on government rules were being criticized before the Asian financial crisis, and they will be seen in the future as imposing high food costs on weaker economies. Japan continues to loosen the government hold on internal rice marketing; Indonesia has announced its intention to dismantle state control of several major commodities; and government-sponsored cooperative federations in several countries are gradually facing more and more competition in providing inputs and in selling outputs. As internal markets become more commercial, exporters will find more opportunities to participate in them.

Government subsidies to agriculture and, in some cases, processing may decline in the next decade. They are considered too expensive in China, South Korea, Japan, and elsewhere. As government subsidies decrease, some domestic production and processing will become less competitive with imports. Subsidies for grain milling, produce marketing, and animal production are examples. However, government subsidies have supported inefficient farms and enterprises and actually weakened the competitiveness of Asian agriculture. An example is government support of small-scale farming, which has made large-scale farming difficult. As those subsidies are reduced, commercial farms may become stronger in parts of Asia.

As trade expands beyond sectors where Asian production is manifestly weak (e.g., cattle, corn, soybeans, cotton, and oranges) to sectors where Asian domestic production is relatively strong, considerable attention will be paid to price. Even modest tariffs will sometimes make the difference between importing or not, if Asian production is relatively competitive. Seasonality and weather fluctuations will mean that trade occurs at certain times or in certain years, but not all the time. The location of food processing may become more of a continuum, so that, depending on wages, exchange rates, and market demand, a firm may produce a larger or smaller proportion of its product in an Asian plant than in a U.S. plant.

The current economic vicissitudes will further heighten Asian sensibility to product price. The confidence that fast rising incomes gave to urban populations throughout Asia in the past decade has been weakened, and a bargain-hunting mentality is replacing the impulse to splurge. On the whole, this should open further opportunities for U.S. agribusiness in Asia, as was demonstrated in Japan in 1994. Preliminary U.S. trade data from 1998, at the height of the crisis, show that consumer-ready exports to South Korea and Southeast Asia have been hard-hit and that such exports have declined at a greater rate than bulk exports in China/Hong Kong and Taiwan. However, in Japan, consumer-ready U.S. exports fell by less than 4 percent in value in the first eight months of 1998, while total agricultural trade fell by over 12 percent. As Japan has shown, economic stagnation (through most of the decade) can coexist with or even foster agricultural trade growth. Even with absolute decline in national income (as in 1998), Japan's imports of consumer-ready agricultural items have dropped very little.

For most Asians, incomes remain too low to be able to frequently purchase consumer-ready foods. When growth returns to most of Asia, this latent demand will present an enormous opportunity for U.S. agricultural exports. As Asia's huge population grows wealthier, consumer-ready foods will be more affordable, and imports from the United States will share in a rising tide of spending on these foods, if trade barriers do not stand in the way. Thus, income prospects for Asia matter greatly to U.S. agriculture.

The experience of the 1990s suggests that U.S. exports of consumer-ready and value-added agricultural products benefited both from income growth in most of Asia and from pressure on incomes in the wealthiest Asian country, Japan. Currently, the strong decline in incomes across much of Asia hurts U.S. consumer-ready exports, but least of all in Japan. If other Asian countries approach Japan's level of economic maturity, U.S. agriculture is likely to find still more markets where demand for its value-added products can grow strongly, even if incomes are not growing. Both the process of economic growth and, through it, the attainment of a high level of wealth offer the promise of strong future growth in agricultural trade with Asia.

5

The Current Financial Instability in Asian Economies

by John H. Andre

Director, Office of Economic Policy,
Bureau of East Asian and Pacific Affairs, U.S. Department of State

The turbulence in Southeast Asia's currency markets began in Thailand on July 2, 1997, when market conditions caused such pressure that the Thai government removed the Thai baht's peg with the U.S. dollar. The markets viewed the exchange rate as unsustainable. The weakness in the baht stemmed from external shocks and regulatory shortcomings. The market focused on Thailand's continued current account deficit of about 8 percent of gross domestic product (GDP), the reduction of heavy capital inflows, and a troubled financial sector. The difficulties in Thailand's financial sector were related to supervision of banks and finance companies and excessive real estate lending. By late 1997, the government had closed or suspended 58 of the country's 91 finance companies.

THE BAD NEWS SPREAD

Periods of currency instability generally spill over to other countries and usually operate through two channels. First, economies in the region are closely linked; trade and investment linkages have significantly increased in the Association of Southeast Asian Nations (ASEAN). Changes in the growth and exchange rates of one economy, like Thailand, inevitably affect its neighbors. Second, during periods of instability, investors tend to look at economies that have conditions similar to those under which the problems began. Economies with large current account deficits and significant growth in property investments are particularly vulnerable to speculative attacks. This was the situation that sparked some of the problems in other Southeast Asian countries.

The attack on the baht spread to other countries. Thailand was quickly followed by the Philippines, which floated its currency. Indonesia and Malaysia appeared to be in better shape at first, but eventually they too were forced to remove their currencies from their peg to the U.S. dollar. In the three-month period from July to September 1997, the Thai baht fell 40

The opinions expressed in this chapter are the author's and do not necessarily reflect those of the U.S. Department of State.

percent against the U.S. dollar. In the same period, the Philippine peso declined 26 percent, the Indonesian rupiah declined 22 percent, and the Malaysian ringgit was down 6 percent. Singapore, in better shape, had its dollar depreciate about 6 percent. Even the Hong Kong dollar came under speculative pressure, but managed to hold its peg to the dollar.

Waves of pressure against the region's currencies have continued. There have been dramatic pressures on the South Korean economy. Statements from some leaders in the region have also depressed markets, which are quick to react when leaders seem to retreat from liberalization and open market policies. Some economies also have lurking political problems, as in Indonesia.

It is difficult to predict how long the current instability will last. During the Mexican peso crisis in 1994-95, the Mexican government was able to attract new capital from private capital markets within a few months after instituting their reforms, which they did with the help of the International Monetary Fund (IMF). Whether South Korea, Thailand, Indonesia, and the Philippines, with similar IMF help, will recover as quickly is an open question.

FOUNDATION FOR FUTURE GROWTH

Financial experts in Asia point out that there is little evidence that exchange rate volatility itself affects long-term trade, investment, or growth rates. Thus, the current period of instability does not necessarily alter the fundamentally bright prospects of the Asian economies. To the extent that the financial crisis resolves currency misalignments and forces countries to adopt needed economic reforms, long-term prospects for the region may actually be enhanced. However, policy adjustments will be difficult. There will be short-term pain, particularly in the economies most affected—Thailand and perhaps the Philippines. There will also be some political activity in looking for scapegoats. It is important to remember that the Asian financial crisis reflects the response of the markets; it was not precipitated by speculators.

The international community responded fairly quickly to the Thai currency instability. In July 1997, the IMF approved an initial $1.1 billion credit for the Philippines, and the Export-Import Bank of Japan (JEXIM) also provided assistance. At that time as well, the IMF approved a $4 billion, 34-month standby arrangement for Thailand, which, together with other countries in the region, received a total package of about $17 billion. Japan was the largest donor; other contributors were Australia, Hong Kong, Indonesia, Malaysia, Singapore, South Korea, the Asian Development Bank, and the World Bank. It is notable that China was involved in a package like this for the first time. The Bank of International Settlements (BIS) made $1 billion available to Thailand to bridge its needs for capital and the beginning of the IMF program. This was the largest IMF program since Mexico's crisis, and Thailand was able to draw up to five times its quota instead of the standard three. Drawings were available up front in recognition of Thailand's immediate needs.

A key element of the program was that the Thai government had to undertake financial sector restructuring, including closing insolvent financial institutions. This was a politically difficult measure to take, and it was not entirely clear how the government would accomplish it.

After eight straight years of a fiscal surplus, in 1997 Thailand had a fiscal deficit, which was one reason that currency speculators turned their attention to that country. As part of the IMF program, the government was obligated to reverse the deficit and achieve a budget surplus by the end of 1997. The government immediately reduced its budget by about 6 percent, maintained a managed float, and expected new financing to roll over its private debt.

Estimates of Thailand's economic growth were reduced from about 7 percent a year to 2.5 percent. It is notable that the other countries in the region, despite their links to Thailand and the effects of the currency instability on their markets, will likely continue in a GDP growth range of 5 to 6 percent (and even 7 percent for Malaysia).

Several officials in the region criticized the United States in the press for its lack of action and participation in the IMF package. However, the United States had been active within the IMF in putting the package together and ensuring that resources were made available to Thailand when they were needed. The United States also provided some of the money for the BIS bridge loan.

RIPPLES FROM THE CURRENCY CRISIS

There are many implications of the major financial difficulties facing the Asian economies. For example, the United States had expected to conclude a financial service agreement in the World Trade Organization by the end of 1997 (a second try), but it had to extend the negotiations. Despite the preoccupation of financial officials with managing the fallout from the currency crisis and despite the tendency of many officials to equate liberalization and opening of markets with increased instability, the United States has made a good case that opening markets and attracting more and longer-term capital will enhance stability and lead to a new financial services agreement.

It is difficult to predict how serious the effect of the Asian financial crisis will be on U.S. agricultural trade. The region's countries are major importers of U.S. agricultural commodities. But if the troubled Asian countries adopt the policies needed to attract more private capital, the crisis can be expected to have little effect on the future for agricultural markets.

6

Regionalism and the Bias Against Agriculture in East Asia

by Dean A. DeRosa

*Principal Economist,
ADR International, Ltd.*

I n this chapter, East Asia refers to the countries of East and Southeast Asia as defined by the World Bank.[1] The region's importance is derived not only from its vast population and diversity of natural and other resources, but also from its sustained high growth of per capita gross domestic product (GDP) and robust export performance during recent decades. This growth has been led by the remarkable economic performance of the newly industrialized countries (NICs)—Hong Kong, Singapore, South Korea, and Taiwan (Table 6-1). Emphasizing the mostly open policies pursued by the NICs, the World Bank has termed the region's economic achievement through the mid-1990s the "East Asian miracle."[2]

Today, East Asia is widely engulfed in the Asian financial crisis that erupted with the floating of the Thai baht in July 1997 and the subsequent decline in East Asia's growth of output and exports. The Asian financial crisis has revealed critical weaknesses in the institutional fabric of many countries in East Asia. In particular, inadequacy of regulatory and prudential controls on banking and financial intermediation, it is argued, has allowed domestic lenders and borrowers in these countries to use short-term international funds to engage in ill-advised long-term investments without concern for fully bearing the risks of unrealizable expectations vested in highly leveraged commercial and industrial projects. This led to reduced confidence by foreign investors, downward pressure on exchange rates, and the current slowdown in East Asia's economic growth and foreign trade (including volume of agricultural imports).[3]

Nonetheless, when ongoing financial policy reforms take hold and economic stability is regained, the populous East Asian region will provide a lucrative market for U.S. farm commodities and products as long as it continues to be governed by increasingly open and liberal economic policies. Trade policies in East Asia—not only for agricultural goods, but also for manufactures and services—are important issues, in addition to economic and political reforms to overcome the spate of recent financial crises. Failure to reduce protection can have significant economywide as well as sectoral impacts, inhibiting more rapid growth and, ultimately, the potential for greater welfare for consumers through the freedom to buy goods from whomever they wish at the lowest price.

45

TABLE 6-1
INDICATORS OF FUNDAMENTAL ECONOMIC FACTORS FOR EAST ASIAN COUNTRIES, 1995

Country	Population Total (Mill.)	Population Density (No./Km²)	Education (Index[b])	Per Capita GNP ($)	Structure of Production Industry (% of GDP)	Structure of Production Agriculture (% of GDP)	Structure of Production Agricultural Labor Force[c] (%)	Growth,[a] 1980-95 GDP (%/Yr.)	Growth,[a] 1980-95 Exports (%/Yr.)
China	1,200	129	82	620	48	21	56	11	12
NICs									
Hong Kong	6	6,252	169	22,990	17	0	0	6	15
Singapore	3	4,896	203	26,730	36	0	0	7	14
South Korea	45	454	333	9,700	43	7	15	9	12
Taiwan[d]	21	583	n.a.	10,850	50	4	11	8	19
Southeast Asia									
Indonesia	193	107	93	980	42	17	51	7	10
Malaysia	20	61	159	3,890	43	13	27[e]	6	14
Philippines	69	230	209	1,050	32	22	46	1	5
Thailand	58	114	132	2,740	40	11	57	8	17

a. In real terms.
b. Index of human resource development calculated as the secondary school enrollment rate plus five times the university enrollment rate, both calculated in their respective age cohorts. Values are for 1993.
c. 1993. As a share of the total domestic labor force.
d. 1980-93 for growth of GDP and exports; 1993 for all other indicators.
e. 1990.

Sources: Asian Development Bank, *Key Economic Indicators of Developing Member Countries of ADB* (Manila, Philippines, 1995); and World Bank, *World Development Indicators 1997* (Washington, DC, 1997).

Protection in the high income NICs is generally lower than protection in the low and middle income countries of East Asia. Nevertheless, not unlike the major industrial countries, the NICs that have more abundant natural resources, South Korea and Taiwan, tend to enforce higher levels of protection against some agricultural goods than against manufactures, reflecting the political influence of small, highly concentrated groups of agricultural producers, particularly rice farmers, in the two countries. This protection significantly limits the ability of U.S. farmers to export greater volumes of fruit, grains, meats, and other food products to these countries, especially to South Korea (and also Japan for similar reasons).

REGIONALISM AND SOUTHEAST ASIA

The structure and political economy of protection differs significantly in China and the countries of Southeast Asia. Although the NICs have largely completed the transition to industrial economies, agriculture still plays a prominent role in the economies of the rest of East Asia, reflecting lower levels of economic development and industrialization. In the lower income countries of East Asia, groups of manufacturers tend to be more concentrated and to recognize their mutual interest in protection from foreign competition. Thus, protection levels tend to be higher for manufactured than for agricultural goods.

Greater protection for manufacturing than for agriculture imparts a bias against agriculture in the lower income countries of East Asia. That is, it tends to repress relative domestic prices for agricultural goods and to cause the real exchange rate to be overvalued. These conditions reduce market incentives for greater and more efficient production (and export) of agricultural goods by competitive farmers in China and Southeast Asia. Studies at the International Food Policy Research Institute (IFPRI), the World Bank, and elsewhere also indicate that the bias against agriculture in less developed countries imposes a significant demand-side constraint on economic growth. The repression of price and other incentives for agriculture causes the purchasing power of rural populations and unskilled urban workers to be lower than otherwise. That is, the bias against agriculture in less developed countries significantly undermines the potential of the agriculture sector to contribute more significantly to macroeconomic growth and national welfare.

Recent economic reforms in China and earlier economic reforms in leading members of the Association of Southeast Asian Nations (ASEAN) have contributed to lessening the bias against agriculture in developing East Asia. (The bias against agriculture is much greater in Africa, for example.) However, considerable scope for greater trade liberalization remains not only in China and the transitional economies of Southeast Asia, e.g., Vietnam, but also in the major ASEAN nations, as is illustrated by the magnitude of the pre-Uruguay Round tariff and nontariff protection statistics for ASEAN countries such as Indonesia, the Philippines, and Thailand in Table 6-2.

ASEAN participated actively in the Uruguay Round of the General Agreement on Tariffs and Trade (GATT) and made substantial commitments under the agreement to liberalize their imports. Beyond the Uruguay

TABLE 6-2
ASEAN IMPORT CONTROL MEASURES, 1987: AVERAGE AD VALOREM TARIFF RATES AND NONTARIFF-BARRIER FREQUENCY RATES* (%)

Imports	Indonesia		Malaysia		Philippines		Singapore		Thailand	
	Tariff	NTB Freq.	Tariff	NTB Freq.	Tariff	NTB Freq.	Tariff	NTB Freq.	Tariff	NTB Freq.
Primary products	15	99	8	5	32	41	0	15	38	24
Foods	25	99	13	6	40	60	0	22	51	37
Cereals	4	100	2	31	42	100	0	31	15	62
Agr. raw materials	10	96	7	6	28	24	0	20	34	15
Crude fertilizers, ores	4	100	4	4	18	13	0	5	19	18
Mineral fuels	5	100	6	0	21	75	2	2	21	11
Nonferrous metals	9	100	7	0	26	0	0	0	25	6
Manufactures	20	93	16	3	34	46	0	14	43	8
Chemicals	11	96	9	3	23	28	0	49	36	6
Iron and steel	8	99	6	8	19	20	0	0	26	8
Machinery and equip.	17	91	12	4	29	88	0	4	33	9
Other manufactures	27	92	22	2	42	28	1	5	51	8
All goods	18	95	14	4	33	45	0	15	41	12

*Tariffs are inclusive of customs' duties and other fiscal charges on imports. Nontariff-barrier frequency rates (NTB freq.) are the percentage of national tariff schedule lines affected by nontariff barriers.

Source: D.A. DeRosa, "Regional Trading Arrangements Among Developing Counties: The ASEAN Example," Research Report 103 (Washington, DC: IFPRI, September 1995).

Round, however, continued liberalization of trade in Southeast Asia has increasingly become intertwined with the "new regionalism" sweeping East Asia and other areas of the world. Indeed, East Asia today is host to the Asia-Pacific Economic Cooperation (APEC) forum, the new ASEAN Free Trade Area (AFTA), and several "growth triangles," e.g., the SIJORI triangle formed by Singapore, Johor (Malaysia), and Riau (Indonesia).

Notwithstanding strong support among policymakers and some economists for the current resurgence of regional trading arrangements, the implications of the new regionalism are not widely known, nor are they known with much certainty. Some economists have emphasized that new cooperative agreements covering trade, investment, and even monetary arrangements among neighboring countries will contribute to deepening economic policy reforms and will strategically strengthen regional economic relations. However, the main ingredient of the new regional trading arrangements remains trade discrimination—that is, the practice of lowering tariffs and other barriers to imports from fellow members of regional trading agreements but not to imports from nonmembers. This violates the cornerstone of GATT—the most-favored-nation (MFN) principle.

THE AFTA PLAN AND SOME QUANTITATIVE RESULTS

IFPRI developed a multisector simulation model to empirically assess the medium-term (i.e., three- to five-year) impacts of AFTA on both economywide and sectoral variables in the five major Southeast Asian countries—Indonesia, Malaysia, the Philippines, Singapore, and Thailand.[4] With this model, IFPRI considered three policy scenarios representing variants of the AFTA plan, announced during 1992-94, and one policy scenario representing MFN trade liberalization.

Under the policy scenarios, the trade restrictions in ASEAN countries in Table 6-2 are reduced on either a discriminatory basis (AFTA scenarios) or a nondiscriminatory basis (MFN scenario). Specifically, the ad valorem tariffs in Table 6-2 are reduced to zero on either a discriminatory or nondiscriminatory basis, while elimination of the nontariff barriers is represented by an increase of 25 percent in the volume of administered imports by ASEAN on either a discriminatory or nondiscriminatory basis.

The simulation results indicate that the AFTA plan is trade-creating on a net basis (Figure 6-1). That is, the plan stimulates greater trade among ASEAN than it diverts from countries outside the agreement. Also, the simulation results indicate that the plan reduces the bias against agriculture in ASEAN that have abundant natural resources—Indonesia, Malaysia, the Philippines, and Thailand, the ASEAN-4. In other words, the plan improves the domestic terms of agricultural trade in the four countries, and it results in expanded agricultural production and exports following the comparative advantage of the four countries in natural resource-based goods and labor-intensive goods (the latter category includes agricultural goods as well as manufactures).

However, the circumstances of agriculture improve substantially less under AFTA than under MFN liberalization (Figure 6-2). Whereas AFTA

FIGURE 6-1

SIMULATED EFFECTS OF AFTA AND MFN
LIBERALIZATION ON TRADE: MEDIUM-TERM
EFFECTS ON TRADE PER ANNUM, BASED ON
1987-88 LEVELS OF IMPORT BARRIERS AND
TRADE FLOWS

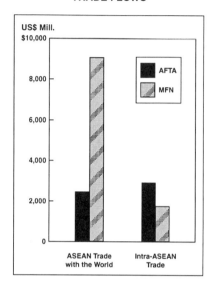

Source: D.A. DeRosa, "Regional Trading Arrangements Among
Developing Countries: The ASEAN Example," Research Report
103 (Washington, DC: IFPRI, September 1995).

results in expanded annual agricultural output from 0.1 percent (Indonesia)
to 0.6 percent (Thailand), MFN liberalization results in expanded annual
agricultural output from 2.3 percent (Indonesia) to 8.7 percent (the Philippines). Similar results are found for the expansion of agricultural exports.

These results reveal the limited potential of AFTA for reducing the bias
against agriculture in Southeast Asia. They also point to other questionable
effects of AFTA, as simulated by this model. Overall, AFTA is estimated to
yield mainly small improvements in national welfare, measured as real
expenditures on final demand (less than 0.5 percent per annum), except in
Singapore and Malaysia. In contrast, liberalizing ASEAN trade on an MFN
basis results in significant gains in economic welfare, ranging from 2 percent
(Indonesia) to about 5 percent (Malaysia and the Philippines). For Singapore, however, economic welfare declines by nearly 2 percent.

In the ASEAN-4, national welfare improves significantly because the
adjustment of consumption and imports as well as of production and exports

FIGURE 6-2

SIMULATED EFFECTS OF AFTA AND MFN LIBERALIZATION ON
AGRICULTURAL PRODUCTION: MEDIUM-TERM EFFECTS ON
AGRICULTURAL OUTPUT PER ANNUM, BASED ON CHANGES
IN AGRICULTURAL OUTPUT BY SUBSECTORS

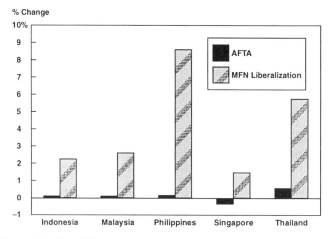

Source: See Figure 6-1.

is consistent with the comparative advantage of the four countries. In other
words, consumers as well as producers in the four countries benefit to the
fullest extent from the freedom provided by nondiscriminatory trade liberalization in both rural and urban areas. For Singapore, the estimated welfare
impact reflects the reduced hegemony of Singapore in regional markets for
manufactures under MFN liberalization. (Under multilateral trade liberalization, Singapore's economic fortunes would be much different because its
economic interest lies in wider multilateral trade liberalization under APEC
or the World Trade Organization.

Finally, although the liberalization of ASEAN trade relations on an
MFN basis results in smaller gains in intra-ASEAN trade ($1.7 billion per
annum), ASEAN trade with the world expands by nearly four times more
under MFN trade liberalization ($9.1 billion) than under AFTA ($2.4 billion). As further evidence that AFTA's potential for reducing policy-based
disincentives to agriculture is only modest, total ASEAN exports of agricultural commodities expand by only about $0.5 billion under AFTA but by
almost $4 billion, or eight times more, under MFN liberalization.

CONCLUSIONS

Regionalism is expected to remain an important factor in international trade relations during the next decade or more. The form regionalism

takes in East Asia, given its prominence in the world economy, could significantly influence the global trading system. Of crucial importance is whether regionalism in East Asia evolves into what has been termed "open regionalism." Open regionalism refers to the liberalization of trade by neighboring countries on a nondiscriminatory or MFN basis. That is, open regionalism would extend regionally agreed reductions in tariffs and non-tariff barriers to all trading partners, without necessarily requiring reciprocal trade concessions from nonregional trading partners. Notably, open regionalism is the stated (but still operationally vague) goal of APEC, but not ASEAN.

The form regionalism takes in East Asia will also significantly influence the agricultural and macroeconomic prospects of the lower income countries in the region. The quantitative findings of the IFPRI simulation model for ASEAN point to the vast superiority of MFN liberalization—or, equivalently, open regionalism—in this regard. The challenges facing the global trading system and the goal of achieving higher sustained growth and economic welfare in developing areas such as Southeast Asia are issues that are central to the international political economy. The problem remains of how the regional trading arrangements arising in East Asia and other areas of the world today can be turned into more enlightened (and faithful) expressions of the MFN principle.

NOTES

1. The World Bank divides Asian countries into East Asia, South Asia, and Central Asia.

2. World Bank, *The East Asian Miracle* (New York: Oxford University Press, 1993).

3. See, for instance, P.R. Krugman, "What Happened to Asia?" Massachusetts Institute of Technology, Cambridge, MA, 1998, mimeo.

4. D.A. DeRosa, *Regional Trading Arrangements Among Developing Counties: The ASEAN Example*, Research Report 103 (Washington, DC: IFPRI, September 1995). See also D.A. DeRosa, "Regionalism and the Bias Against Agriculture in Less-Developed Countries," in *The World Economy: Global Trade Policy 1996* (supplement volume to *The World Economy*), ed. S. Arndt and C. Milner (Cambridge, MA: Blackwell Publishers, 1996).

7

Impact of the Asian Financial Crisis on U.S. Agricultural Exports

by Michael J. Dwyer

International Economist, Commodity and Marketing Programs, Foreign Agricultural Service, U.S. Department of Agriculture

I n the six months following July 1997, the currencies of four Southeast Asian nations (Indonesia, Malaysia, the Philippines, and Thailand) and South Korea fell by 40 to 70 percent against the U.S. dollar, precipitating a financial and economic crisis that continues to threaten U.S. agricultural exports. South Korea, Indonesia, and Thailand sought assistance from the International Monetary Fund (IMF), which responded with loan programs totaling $100 billion. With Southeast Asia and South Korea accounting for 12 percent of total U.S. agricultural exports, any significant decline in exports to these markets will have serious implications for the United States and other major exporting nations, whose farm prices are already feeling the effects of reduced demand. This chapter addresses how the crisis is likely to affect U.S. agricultural exports and how the credit programs of the IMF and the U.S. Department of Agriculture (USDA) help mitigate the impact of the crisis on producers.

GLOBAL IMPACTS

In FY1998, the Asian financial crisis is estimated to have reduced worldwide U.S. agricultural exports by $2 billion, or 3.4 percent, from levels that would have prevailed had there been no crisis. The impacts of the crisis are expected to intensify in FY1999 as the sharply slowing economic growth or outright recession in Asian countries results in more significant reductions in their import demand, while the appreciation of the U.S. dollar, relative to U.S. competitors' currencies, more negatively affects U.S. market share. However, after FY1999, the trade impacts will likely begin to ease as Asian currencies, economies, and import demand start to recover.

These estimates take into account the trade and economic stabilization benefits of the IMF loan programs in Indonesia, South Korea, and Thailand. However, they do not include the potentially offsetting impacts of the $2.5

The views expressed in this chapter are the author's and do not necessarily represent the views of the USDA.

billion export-credit guarantee programs of the USDA for South Korea and Southeast Asia (see "Benefits of USDA Export-Credit Guarantee Programs," page 56).

These impacts for 1998 and 1999 were based on estimates made in January 1998. The assumptions used then regarding the outlook for Asian economic growth and currencies called for sharply slowing or zero rates of growth but no recessions in the nations of the region. Because we now know that much of Asia is in recession in 1998 and will continue to be in 1999, the trade impact estimates appear too conservative. Nonetheless, the estimates still show the seriousness of the crisis and their new impacts on U.S. exports.

Despite short-term disruptions, the long-term outlook for the region's economies and trade with the United States remains favorable if the governments undertake needed macroeconomic reforms. The most affected countries have well-educated and highly productive workforces, flexible economies, and generally well-developed infrastructures. This is no reason to believe that these economies cannot recover much of their past rapid growth. However, should the Asian crisis deepen and become a global crisis, the impacts on U.S. exports could be even greater. Three possible developments would be cause for serious concern: A currency devaluation by China to maintain its export competitiveness with the rest of Asia; a financial meltdown in Japan; or the spread of the financial crisis to Latin America.

COUNTRY IMPACTS

Of the $2 billion decline in estimates of U.S. global agricultural exports for FY1998, 80 percent is in Asia (Table 7-1). Particularly hard hit will be shipments to South Korea and Southeast Asia, which are projected to be $1.25 billion lower than the pre-crisis estimate for 1998. While some observers have expressed concern over Japan's financial problems, others believe the situation in Japan is more stable and unlikely to reach the crisis stage. As a result, estimates of U.S. agricultural exports to Japan shrink less than 2 percent, or $200 million. Likewise, little impact is expected on U.S. agricultural exports to China and Hong Kong, which do not appear to be greatly affected by the financial storms that surround them. The drop in exports to those two markets totals roughly $100 million.

Given the global nature of this crisis, estimates of U.S. agricultural exports to non-Asian markets fall as well, although by only 1.3 percent, or $400 million. These losses will result primarily from lower U.S. crop and livestock prices because of reduced demand in Asia and will affect the value of exports regardless of destination.

COMMODITY IMPACTS

Approximately two-thirds of the $2 billion drop in exports for FY1998 are in high value products, which are more price- and income-sensitive than bulk commodities (Table 7-2). The decline in estimates for high value products is led by horticultural products and red meats and poultry, which account for $400 million each. However, in FY1999, the negative impact on

TABLE 7-1

IMPACT OF THE ASIAN FINANCIAL CRISIS ON U.S. GLOBAL AGRICULTURAL EXPORTS BY COUNTRY, 1997 and 1998 (US$ MILL.)

Export Destination	FY1997 Actual	FY1998 Estimates		Change in FY1998 Est.
		Pre-Crisis*	Revised	
South Korea	3,283	3,400	2,900	− 500
ASEAN	3,073	3,170	2,420	− 750
Indonesia	767	790	540	− 250
Malaysia	580	600	450	− 150
Philippines	893	920	770	− 150
Singapore	284	300	250	− 50
Thailand	549	560	410	− 150
Japan	10,697	10,900	10,700	− 200
China/Hong Kong	3,406	3,300	3,200	− 100
Taiwan	2,582	2,400	2,300	− 100
Other	34,183	35,830	35,430	− 400
World	57,224	59,000	56,950	−2,050

*The December 2, 1997, *Outlook for U.S. Agricultural Exports* estimated the impact of the Asian financial crisis in FY1998 at $500 million and worldwide exports at $58.5 billion, implying that without the crisis, U.S. exports would have been $59 billion. Therefore, the pre-crisis estimate restores this $500 million.

Source: USDA, *Outlook for U.S. Agricultural Exports* (December 2, 1997).

bulk commodity exports will likely become more pronounced as Asian economies slow further and competitors benefit from an appreciating U.S. dollar. U.S. producers are projected to respond to lower crop prices by slightly lowering production. As a result, the value of wheat, coarse grains, soybeans, and cotton exports is estimated to decline by more than 6 percent in FY1999 (compared with pre-crisis baseline estimates) before recovering in 2000 and 2001.

STRATEGIC RESPONSES MITIGATING THE IMPACTS

Two factors will bear heavily on the final impact of the Asian crisis: The success of the IMF's programs in stabilizing and restructuring the economies of the affected countries; and USDA's export-credit guarantee programs.

Benefits of IMF Programs

The Asian crisis marks the second time in three years (the Mexican peso crisis that broke out in 1994 was the first) that large IMF programs have

TABLE 7-2

IMPACT OF THE ASIAN FINANCIAL CRISIS ON U.S. GLOBAL AGRICULTURAL EXPORTS BY COMMODITY, 1997 and 1998 (US$ MILL.)

Commodity	FY1997 Actual	FY1998 Estimates Pre-Crisis	FY1998 Estimates Revised	Change in FY1998 Est.
Coarse grains	6,921	7,500	7,375	− 125
Soybeans and products	8,696	8,100	7,850	− 250
Wheat and flour	4,263	4,600	4,500	− 100
Cotton	2,737	2,800	2,625	− 175
Beef, pork, and poultry	7,071	7,800	7,400	− 400
Horticulture	10,598	11,200	10,800	− 400
Other	16,974	17,000	16,400	− 600
Total	57,260	59,000	56,950	−2,050

Source: See Table 7-1.

been implemented in markets where the United States has strategic agricultural interests. In the short term, the IMF-mandated trade and investment reforms in the affected countries are helping to steady the uncertain financial environment. Financial stability is critical for commercial trade. Letters of credit are among the first casualties of financial instability, and without them, agricultural exports are greatly impaired.

In the long term, IMF-mandated trade liberalization measures should benefit competitive producers in the United States and elsewhere by ensuring the implementation of structural reforms that will allow imported products greater access to these markets on a permanent basis. Structural reforms include measures to provide greater transparency in customs procedures and other government activities. A number of specific reforms relating to agriculture are also included. For example, in Indonesia, tariffs on imported food have been reduced from a 20-40 percent rate to a maximum rate of only 5 percent. Also, BULOG, Indonesia's state-owned exclusive importer of many agricultural products, is being substantially reformed. This should help to boost U.S. exports of wheat and soybeans in that country.

The 3-6 percent loss estimates cited above take into account the positive impacts that are expected from the IMF loan programs in South Korea, Indonesia, and Thailand. If the IMF programs were not in place, the negative impact on U.S. agricultural exports would likely be greater.

Benefits of USDA Export-Credit Guarantee Programs

To help mitigate the negative impacts of the crisis on U.S. exporters, USDA has approved more than $2.5 billion in export-credit guarantees to be used in South Korea and Southeast Asia. There is substantial disagreement among economists about the additional exports likely to be realized from extending credit guarantees to these countries. Some argue that the additions will be fairly low because these countries are highly dependent on food imports. Others argue that the additions will be high because the guarantees provide a strong psychological impetus to the private sector and to governments to maintain imports, they somewhat mitigate the lack of liquidity brought on by the crisis, and they attract customers for whom credit is a critical factor in determining purchases. As noted above, the estimates in this chapter do not include the partially offsetting impacts of the credit guarantees.

8

Prospects for Economic Growth in East Asia

by Will Martin

Principal Economist,
Development Research Group, World Bank

We are living in interesting times. The world is being reshaped by the interplay of trade and open markets and investment in physical capital and in people. Profound changes are under way in global markets for agricultural products and in the world economy in general. This chapter discusses some of the implications of the rapid and uneven changes that are occurring, particularly in Asia.

DECLINING WORLD FOOD PRICES

The recent history of world food prices has been exactly the opposite of what Malthus, a leading early exponent of the dismal science of economics, propounded. There has been a consistent downward trend in real food prices, albeit with considerable variation around this trend. This is remarkable because all the conditions that Malthus pointed to in arguing that food prices would inexorably rise have come to pass: Geometric population growth has enormously increased world population; and land constraints are now binding worldwide with the closing of the land frontier in most countries. In addition, there has been substantial outmigration from agriculture in rich countries, particularly in the high growth economies of East Asia where the share of labor in agriculture in output has been dropping rapidly. Nevertheless, diets, on average, have improved dramatically. In recent years, considerable improvement has taken place at the bottom of the income chain, as millions of people have been lifted out of poverty, especially in East Asia.

Two key factors explain the decline in food prices: Food demand grows less rapidly than income; and agricultural technology has improved. World Bank data show that the tendency for a sharp downward move in prices has existed since early this century. But in the past few years, some experts have predicted a new era in which world food prices would soar. One argument has been that China's import demand would result in exorbitantly high world food prices, starving the rest of the world.[1] However, the historical record and recent price movements speak against this conclusion.

A MODEL OF THE GLOBAL ECONOMY

In collaboration with Purdue University and the University of Adelaide, the World Bank has undertaken an analysis of the changing structure of the world economy for the years 1992 to 2005, a period long enough for substantial changes to occur in the size and structure of individual economies.[2] A general equilibrium model with different income elasticities and factor intensities by sector was used. As the world economy expands and capital is accumulated, the model shows realistic structural changes. Although the rapid growth of developing East Asia has suffered setbacks because of the financial crisis beginning in 1997, growth will likely be resumed over the longer period. The changes include substantial increases in agricultural imports from developing countries and continued growth of some East Asian agricultural export markets for the United States. The real price decline that has been built into the analysis will continue in line with the World Bank's forecasts of real food prices.

The World Bank's projections for 1992-2005 show much higher economic growth rates than in the past in some of the high growth economies of East Asia. China's growth rate is estimated at about 8 percent per year for the period, resulting in total growth of over 150 percent. A lower growth rate of 129 percent is projected for South Korea and for Indonesia. Thailand's cumulative growth rate is projected to be 173 percent. A more recent forecast would show only somewhat lower percentages because Asia's current financial difficulties appear to be a relatively short-term downturn on a long-term growth path.

The contrast between these growth rates and those of North America and Europe, where growth rates are projected to average 2.6 percent and 2.5 percent per year respectively, points to dramatic changes in the structure of the world economy, particularly over even longer periods. In the World Bank's *Global Economic Prospects 1997*, the world share of Chinese exports is estimated to expand from about 4 percent in 1997 to almost 10 percent in 2020.[3]

ESCALATING GROWTH OF CAPITAL STOCK

Changes in the structure of demand for agricultural products will result from rapid income growth. The future of the high growth economies of East Asia is tied to high savings rates. Savings rates in China have increased from over 40 percent of gross domestic product (GDP) to approximately 45 percent in recent years. When incomes rise at near double-digit levels per year, as was the case for many of the high growth East Asian countries during the first half of the 1990s, and savings increase to 40-45 percent of GDP, capital stock expands very rapidly. Numerous variations will occur, depending on the savings rates and the extent to which individual East Asian economies draw on foreign savings. But the Bank projects exceptional growth rates of capital stock in these countries—much higher than in the North American economies or any other advanced industrial nation.

The growth of capital also depends on foreign savings. The use of foreign savings in developing countries is rapidly increasing. *Global Economic Prospects* reports an enormous growth in private capital inflows into these economies, from about 1 percent of GDP in 1991 to 4.5 percent in 1996.

Private capital inflows not only contribute to the growth of total capital, but they also enable the introduction of advanced techniques and ideas that support the faster growth of developing countries.

The extraordinary increase of capital stock relative to that of the labor force will dramatically impact the structure of the high growth East Asian economies. In trade theory, if both a capital-intensive and a labor-intensive sector exist in the economy and if additional capital becomes available, the capital-intensive sector will grow and the labor-intensive sector will shrink. When more capital becomes available in a capital-intensive industrial sector—for example, first apparel and then transport and machinery—jobs will be created in that sector, drawing resources away from agriculture. It is not urbanization that draws resources away from agriculture, but the increasing availability of capital-intensive and skill-intensive jobs.

CHANGING THE IMPORT/EXPORT MIX

The GTAP global general equilibrium model used in the study shows that these factors have a large impact on the structure of the global economy. First, a baseline simulation examined the growth of capital, labor, education, human capital, and productivity. Then, their impact was traced on the patterns of growth and trade (in constant 1992 dollars). For example, given the projections model and its underlying assumptions, China's trade deficit in agricultural products—grains, soybeans, oilseeds, and vegetables—is projected to expand during the 1992-2005 period. The model reflects the fact that, within agriculture, demand growth is more rapid in products that have higher income elasticities such as fruits and vegetables than in basic grains, which received considerable attention in *Who Will Feed China?*[4] China is expected to pay for growing food imports with exports from the manufacturing sector, with very rapid growth in exports in more advanced sectors such as transport and machinery. In addition, China's apparel exports will greatly expand in the period to 2005. Although they are more capital-intensive than agriculture, they are held back by the Multi-Fiber Arrangement (MFA), which has not been abolished for China as it will be for members of the World Trade Organization (WTO). In the Bank's simulation, the Association of Southeast Asian Nations (ASEAN) takes up some of the slack in apparel exports, which will rapidly increase with the termination of the MFA. The simulation is somewhat artificial because the date of China's admittance to the WTO is not known, but it seems likely to occur at some point within the time frame of the projections.

POLICY SCENARIOS

"May you live in interesting times" is an ancient Chinese curse and one we seem destined to experience. The World Bank considered several factors that potentially could go wrong and some that could go right and developed the following policy scenarios.

Arable Land Loss

One scenario involved the potential loss of agricultural land. This issue—for example, the idea of paving over rice fields to cope with urbanization—has received considerable attention in terms of China and other East Asian economies. The analysis incorporated data reflecting the rapid expansion of urban populations, urban density, and the consequences of losing agricultural land. When the amount of land that might be used for urbanization was compared with the total arable land by country, extremely small numbers resulted. Indeed, the impact was so slight that the simulation was uninteresting.

Declining Agricultural Productivity

There have been considerable national and international efforts to improve technology in agriculture. These undertakings have been successful, and productivity in agriculture has been growing more rapidly in most countries than productivity in the industrial sector or the rest of the economy. However, because of signs of fatigue in the funding of international agricultural research, the possibility of a slowdown in technical change in agriculture was also examined.

Based on an estimated 2.5 percent a year growth rate in total factor productivity in grain during the past 20 years, the simulation explored the impact of reducing total factor productivity growth by 0.5 percent a year. Over the 13-year period from 1992 to 2005, substantial increases in the prices of agricultural products are projected—much larger than the increases that were estimated to arise from the Uruguay Round of the General Agreement on Tariffs and Trade and that caused so much controversy at the time. The income losses could become enormous, hitting poor people for whom food is the major part of their consumption spending.

Influence of the Multi-Fiber Arrangement

Another scenario evaluated the abolition of the MFA scheduled for 2005. It is worrisome that the serious liberalization under the MFA—dismantling almost one-half of the quotas and all of the important ones—has been deferred to the end of the 10-year phase-out period. This simulation incorporated the MFA restrictions on agricultural products. ASEAN, which will be heavily dependent on its textile and clothing exports by 2005, will have to find additional exports and will turn to agriculture. This then reduces the scope for increases in agricultural exports from the North American Free Trade Agreement. In other words, everything depends on everything else, and some of these linkages are strong and significant.

Slower Growth In China

A slowdown in China's growth would slow the process of pulling resources out of agriculture, thus increasing China's agricultural exports. Of course, agricultural exports to China would fall because it would be producing more food, and demanding less.

China's Accession to the WTO

One scenario looked at the actual offers that China had on the table in early 1997 for the WTO accession negotiations. Even though there was little liberalization in agriculture in the offers considered, the final terms of accession will likely involve considerably more liberalization—subsequent offers by China during 1997 and 1998 have already included significantly more liberalization. However, the simulation provides some indication of the nature of the liberalization. There will be substantial increases in real income in China and in its major trading partners, including those in North America. Some East Asian countries that compete in product range with China are likely to suffer losses because of China's liberalization associated with WTO entry.

CONCLUSION

Rapid changes are occurring in the world economy, particularly in East Asia. These changes will alter world trade, with a marked impact on agricultural trade. It is critical that agricultural research and development continue at the same pace. In considering agricultural trade with China and in general, it is important to look beyond grain trade. Grain trade is likely to remain a relatively small part of future growth. Finally, changes in the nonfood area and in trade policy in general will have a significant impact, for good or ill, on agricultural trade.

NOTES

1. Lester Brown, *Who Will Feed China? Wake Up Call for a Small Planet* (New York: Norton, 1995).

2. K. Anderson, B. Dimaranan, T. Hertel, and W. Martin, "Economic Growth and Policy Reform in the APEC Region: Trade and Welfare Implications by 2005," *Asia-Pacific Economic Review*, Vol. 3, No.1, pp. 1-19; and K. Anderson, B. Dimaranan, T. Hertel, and W. Martin, "Asia-Pacific Food Markets and Trade in 2005: A Global, Economy-wide Perspective," *Australian Journal of Agricultural and Resource Economics*, Vol. 41, No. 1, pp. 19-44.

3. World Bank, *Global Economic Prospects and the Developing Countries 1997* (Washington, DC, 1997).

4. Brown, *Who Will Feed China?*

PART III

THE POTENTIAL FOR GROWTH IN TRADE AND INVESTMENT— THE PRIVATE SECTOR VIEW

9

The Potential for U.S. Food and Agricultural Trade in East and Southeast Asia

by Robbin S. Johnson

*Corporate Vice President, Public Affairs,
Cargill, Incorporated*

T he potential for U.S. food and agricultural trade in East and Southeast Asia will be shaped by four factors: resource endowments; economic trends within the region; East and Southeast Asian policy decisions; and U.S. policy measures that might affect those decisions. The last two issues are the ones most subject to influence. Formulating policy that encourages market-based reforms would help to create an open Asian food system.

RESOURCE CONSTRAINTS

Four resource considerations are particularly important for Asia's food situation. First, Asia has a high ratio of labor to land. In fact, the population per arable hectare in Asia is six times that in the Western Hemisphere. Second, rural job creation would be accelerated by a shift from grains to more labor-intensive crops. In China, for example, producing fruits and vegetables takes 4.5 times as much labor per hectare as producing grains. Third, there is substantial underinvestment in Asia's food and agricultural infrastructure to the extent that there are deficiencies in every aspect of the handling and distribution system. Asia's food distribution system over the next 25 years needs to grow 100 to 150 percent, which will increase the demand for capital and new technologies in food distribution. Finally, East and Southeast Asia will account for three-fifths of the world's population growth between now and 2010. The region will also experience almost one-half of the global economy's income growth during that period. The Asian demand for food will grow, straining local production capabilities and the environment.

REGIONAL ECONOMIC TRENDS

These resource constraints are likely to be aggravated by regional economic trends. Asia's yearly gross domestic product (GDP) growth rates were in the range of 7.5 percent per year until the financial crisis struck in July 1997. To restore growth to a high level, some changes are necessary, including greater deregulation and more balanced macroeconomic policies. While these adjustments will be painful, they appear likely to occur in most countries of the region.

Asia is undergoing the most rapid urbanization in human history, which requires much more complex food distribution and handling systems. East and Southeast Asia's growth also has been trade-led to a greater degree than the growth of many other regions that have been industrialized. Asian economies have benefited from and been reshaped by trade liberalization, and their future economic growth depends on continuing and extending market reforms.

Another trend that will become more visible in the future, assuming high growth rates are restored, is the challenge of social stratification. India, for example, has 250 million people who are classified as middle class in global terms, but it also has more than 500 million people who live in poverty.

Income-driven shifts in Asian dietary patterns will become increasingly important to the region's trade potential. As incomes rise, people diversify their diets by shifting the source of calories away from staples and toward foods such as fruits and vegetables, animal protein, fats and oils, and sweeteners. For example, over the past 20 years, world grain and rice consumption has risen 44 percent, but world meat consumption has increased 62 percent, protein meal consumption has grown 114 percent, and vegetable oil consumption has expanded 141 percent. The result is that diets have become more varied and resource-intensive.

ASIA'S POLICY OPTIONS

Oversimplifying somewhat, four policy decisions face East and Southeast Asia in the coming years that will have important individual and cumulative effects on the agricultural trade of the region. First, what agricultural development strategy will these nations choose? Will they choose self-sufficiency in production of staples? Or will they shift their agricultural development toward serving rising dietary expectations through specialization along the lines of comparative advantage?

Second, what will be their approach to rural development? Historically, countries have pursued rural development by trying to combat agriculture's declining terms of trade through price and income supports and related efforts to manage agricultural production and distribution. This approach tends to yield imbalances in production patterns, inefficiencies within the agricultural system as a whole, and unintended adverse consequences for the larger economy. As an alternative, Asian countries have the opportunity to develop a policy of much more market-based diversification of their rural economies. This will require them to invest in infrastructure and job opportunities in rural areas. This type of policy would foster more vital rural economies and higher rates of growth in agricultural productivity.

The third policy decision concerns trade strategy. Asia must choose between a mercantilist approach that promotes exports and retards imports or a trade-liberalizing approach that concentrates on eliminating barriers and opening up two-way trade flows.

Fourth, Asia faces an investment strategy choice. One option is to retain a high degree of state ownership and control in the economy (the failed socialist model from which many of these countries are struggling to escape). The other option is a more market-oriented approach that opens the economies to domestic and foreign investment.

Among these policy areas—agricultural development, rural development, trade, and investment—are obviously many potential combinations of policy choices. But oversimplifying again allows a focus on two extremes. At one extreme, Asia could end up with a food system that is essentially based on nation-states—oriented toward self-sufficiency in staples and with highly interventionist policies in agriculture and rural areas. The resulting trade strategy would be mercantilist, and the investment strategy would severely limit participation by foreigners in Asian economies. If Asian countries make these choices, the result will be a much slower rate of economic growth for the region, with serious strains on the region's environmental resources and a higher level of political instability.

Until the financial crisis that began in 1997, Asia appeared to be moving away from that strategy. But the fallout from recent events in exchange and financial markets calls into question the Asian governments' commitment to reform.

The other extreme would actually accelerate the region's movement toward a more open approach to economic development. It would embrace specialization of local agricultural systems along the lines of comparative resource endowments, more diversified rural economies, and open trade and investment policies. This, in effect, was the policy mix to which these countries committed themselves in the Bogor Declaration of 1994. Unfortunately, this policy is more theory than reality so far, and the real question for the Asia-Pacific region in the next few years is how much substance it can bring to that commitment.

U.S. POLICY DECISIONS

The United States is a member of the Pacific Rim community, and thus its decisions can directly and positively affect Asia's future policies. Two decisions would be particularly beneficial. First, is the United States prepared to join the Asian community in bringing down trade and investment barriers? This has been a neglected part of the fast track debate, which has focused more on hemispheric and global trade negotiations. But fast track authority could be important in spurring trade liberalization in the Asia-Pacific Economic Cooperation (APEC) countries.

Unlike the typical negotiating framework, APEC proceeds more on the basis of community consensus. This means, particularly for the food and agricultural sector, that progress toward liberalization can occur even if a few countries resist change. Japan and South Korea have strongly resisted opening their food and agricultural systems, but that is not necessarily how other countries in the region may come to see food trade.

Table 9-1 illustrates an interesting fact: Among the principle countries of APEC, most are net food exporters. Only Japan, Korea, and Hong Kong have large food deficits. Thus, the vast majority of these countries could regard rapidly lowering food and agricultural trade barriers not simply as opening their economies to greater import dependence, but also as a way of expanding opportunities for marketing their own food and agricultural exports. This is a very different dynamic than that in traditional agricultural negotiations and deserves to be aggressively pursued.

TABLE 9-1

FOOD AND LIVE ANIMAL IMPORTS AND EXPORTS, 1995
(US$ BILL.)

Country	Imports	Exports	Net Exports[a]
Australia	2.2	9.7	7.5
Canada	8.2	11.5	3.3
Chile	0.8	3.5	2.7
China	6.1	9.9[b]	3.8
Hong Kong	7.5	2.7	(4.8)
Indonesia	3.0	3.6	0.6
Japan	45.7	1.6	(44.1)
Malaysia	3.1	1.8	(1.3)
Mexico	3.2	5.4	2.2
New Zealand	0.8	5.6	4.8
Philippines	2.1	1.3	(0.8)
Singapore	3.6	2.5	(1.1)
South Korea	5.9	2.6	(3.3)
Thailand	2.2	10.7	8.5
United States	29.3	42.2	12.9

a. Parentheses indicate that imports exceeded exports.

b. Just four categories—fruits, vegetables, meats, and canned foods—represented $5.5 billion of China's 1995 food exports. Those four categories have quadrupled in value since 1981 and reflect resource endowments that suggest sustainable trade advantages.

Source: United Nations, *1995 International Trade Statistics Yearbook*, Vol. I, Trade by Country (New York, 1996).

The second decision is whether the United States is prepared to assure access to supplies in exchange for greater access to markets. As the leader of the free world, the United States has used unilateral economic sanctions for short-supply reasons, for foreign policy reasons, and most recently in response to domestic political pressures to pursue certain values such as human rights and environmental protection. The frequent threat of unilateral economic sanctions has made assured access to supplies a vital issue for all Asian countries that, as a result of opening their systems, would have to import more grains and oilseeds.

Traditionally, concern about import dependence is presented as concern about food security. Countries fear that a sudden decline in domestic production would leave them too dependent on grain imports as a staple in their diet. To protect against this outcome, countries often pursue expensive self-sufficiency strategies, including, as in China, treatment of food stocks as a national security issue.

Within a country, production can vacillate as much as 25 percent in a given year. Because annual stockholding costs are 20 to 25 percent of the value of the commodity, the expense of holding sufficient stocks to offset potentially large local production swings mounts quickly.

Globally, however, production swings are much smaller, typically 3 to 5 percent per year. Relying on trade flows rather than stocks to address food security concerns would dramatically reduce the unit cost of providing a given level of supply assurance or price stability. Because of resource constraints in most Asian countries, this would be an enormously important economic savings.

The traditional food security concern also fails to take into account changing dietary expectations brought on by income growth. As rising incomes push Asian countries toward more varied diets, grain and oilseed imports are not just a dietary staple, but are also the raw materials for an increasingly important part of their economies, the animal protein chain. In other words, economic development shifts the terms of the debate from emotional concerns about food security to economic interests in food reliability.

For the Asia-Pacific economic region to develop as a successful economic and political community, it must satisfy both food security and food reliability concerns. This puts the goal of self-sufficiency in a new light. China could remain about 95 percent self-sufficient in grains over the medium term simply by making large investments to close the gap between its yields and the highest yields globally, as well as investments in infrastructure that lower post-harvest losses from their current 5-7 percent levels. But this strategy will not equip China, or any other country, to provide reliable food supplies as rising incomes create demand for diversifying diets beyond the essentials. For that kind of food reliability, a new policy approach is needed.

That new policy approach for Asia's food and agricultural system is structured on a different paradigm than the experience of western Europe. The new paradigm is organized around:

1. Aligning domestic prices with world prices to facilitate a shift toward specialization along the lines of comparative advantage and to meet rising expectations for more diverse diets;

2. Embracing open trade and investment policies to build the efficient input and output handling, processing, and distribution systems that will be required;

3. Pursuing a rural development strategy based on comparative resource endowments, especially by encouraging labor-intensive forms of development that will promote both high-value agriculture and the growth of off-farm job opportunities in rural areas; and

4. Guaranteeing access to supplies on a nondiscriminatory basis, both to remove the traditional food security concerns and to create a free-flowing system of investment capital and goods that will lead to the highly specialized, interconnected regional food system that Asia requires for the 21st century.

This paradigm could be a transforming force for the Asia-Pacific region. Food imports would constitute an increasing share of the diets of the Asian region as a whole, based on an expansion in both imports and exports of food. China, for example, would import more grains and oilseeds and export more fruits and vegetables, fish, and animal protein products. It would import to meet its own population needs and to supply value-added foodstuffs on a much larger scale to its Asian neighbors.

This interconnected, efficient, dynamic, and open regional food system would contribute to higher living standards throughout Asia. It would also expand markets for U.S. exports of grains, oilseeds, meats, dairy products, and horticultural goods. Perhaps most important, by uniting the region around its pressing food problem, the food system would become more environmentally sound and would create a more stable, cohesive political community in Asia.

10

Competition, Cooperation, and Competitive Advantage

by Richard Gilmore

*President and Chief Executive Officer,
GIC Trade, Inc.*

U. S. agricultural trade and investment are changing radically. Clearly, U.S. agricultural markets are expanding, bringing new challenges. The unique characteristics of Asian countries in particular challenge the industry and must be considered in conjunction with the changing nature of agricultural trade worldwide. Current data point favorably to increasing market share for U.S. agricultural exports and products until 2005, when the growth rate of bulk commodities is expected to taper off.

INCREASING COMPETITION

Liberalization means increased competition. However, although competition is trade-creating, it does not necessarily translate into increased trade flows as measured by U.S. current accounts in the balance of payments. Liberalization creates tougher competition for growing markets from foreign suppliers as well as local suppliers.

Increasing competition in the food industry is a global issue. In 1994, only 19 countries accounted for 89 percent of all manufactured food imports, while 80 percent of all international shipments originated in just 24 countries. In 1990, the leading suppliers of food were France, Germany, the Netherlands, the United Kingdom, and the United States, accounting for approximately 38 percent of the total. Food manufacturers in these countries have made major acquisitions, resulting in a high level of concentration in the industry and a growing affiliate network in Asia. Despite the slowdown in the Asian economies that has arisen from the crisis beginning in 1997, foreign-owned companies will be well positioned to capture more of that market in the future. They will also benefit from the shift in exchange rates, in favor of parent companies, which should result in cheaper product sourcing for third-country markets.

Competition is indeed important to the United States. U.S. sales of food by foreign affiliates are an increasingly significant component of the changing structure and integrated nature of agricultural trade and have been expanding by about 25 percent a year since 1990. It is clear that investment tends to generate trade and that affiliate relationships are market-creating. Foreign affiliates with investments in the United States generate more trade than U.S. companies with affiliates overseas. Therefore, investment in Asia needs to be critically assessed to increase the efficiency and scope of U.S. food sales in that region.

TARGETED LIBERALIZATION

By allowing graduated schedules for the reduction of trade restrictions, the guidelines of the World Trade Organization (WTO) have resulted in targeted and unsynchronized forms of liberalization. No doubt, the need for an international agreement necessitated this realistic approach. However, from the private sector standpoint, targeted liberalization may be compounded by unregulated substitution policies for investment, especially concerning agricultural projects.

Aside from the attendant intricacies of interpreting policy inconsistencies and regulatory biases, many larger emerging markets pose particular problems for foreign food manufacturers. The biggest single problem is inadequate infrastructure for transportation, distribution, and handling. Other inefficiencies involve cultural and policy considerations such as incomplete privatization in former socialist countries and protectionist trade and investment policies in countries like India. For example, although the affiliate of GIC Trade, Inc. in Bombay is becoming a profit center after five years of operation, significant hurdles remain, attributable in large part to the selective nature of targeted liberalization and the resultant absence of uniformity and transparency in many reform measures.

The challenge for the United States is how to tap into the sizable emerging markets like India to participate in their growth. China (the seventh largest economy in the world) constitutes the third largest trading partner of the United States, its fourth largest export market, and its third largest supplier. India is one of the world's largest agricultural producers, but processes less than 5 percent of its output. Vast quantities spoil before reaching the consumer, with loss ratios as shockingly high as 30 percent. In both countries, a stark need exists for agricultural inputs and the "soft side"of the industry—information and technical services. The latter constitute around 20 percent of U.S. agricultural exports worldwide. Nowhere is the need for their application greater than in China and India.

EXPANDING STRATEGIES TO INCLUDE
THE ENTIRE SYSTEM

It is important that agriculture not be characterized as being merely the flow of products. Products can no longer be regarded separately as bulk, intermediate, or processed; rather, the entire system from origination to delivery must be considered. To penetrate Asian markets or increase market share, the United States needs to examine the whole picture. Opportunities in the region will continue for U.S. agricultural companies, even though the competition is stiff and market access is problematic at this time.

Market Entry

There is no single roadmap for market entry in emerging markets. In fact, directions are even less clear today given the volatility in Asian and Latin American markets. Nonetheless, it is an opportune time to develop a marketing and investment strategy for these countries. The obvious prerequisite for gaining a foothold in these markets is to establish a presence. However, the presence may take several forms, from a strategic alliance to actual foreign direct investment (FDI). For example, in Thailand, many U.S. firms choose to form joint ventures with Thai partners because of their familiarity with the Thai economy and local regulations. But Japanese and European firms understand the Thai business environment better than do Americans, exhibiting considerable flexibility and willingness to do business the "Thai way." They also maximize their use of financing, quality control, and customer service. Hence, the U.S. share of foreign investment in Thailand is only 16 percent.

Government policies in Singapore encourage local firms to form strategic partnerships, especially in high technology activities. There are no taxes on capital gains and no restrictions on foreign ownership of businesses. Foreign investors are not required to take on private or official joint ventures or cede management control at the local level. The most serious investment barriers are complicated specifications regarding foreign ownership and control of companies.

In the Philippines, some barriers exist that make market entry difficult, including quantitative restrictions on more than 100 agricultural and industrial items. The United States is the Philippines' largest trading partner in terms of overall trade turnover, and traditionally it has been the Philippines' top supplier. Recently, however, Japanese investment has outpaced U.S. investment in the Philippines.

Although one of the most imperiled markets, Malaysia continues to offer opportunities for U.S. agriculture. In FY1996, Malaysia imported $10.8 billion of goods and services from Japan and more than $8.5 billion from the United States. To succeed in the Malaysian market, U.S. firms would be best served by establishing themselves in the market and forming relationships with local companies. This strategy, in some part, could apply to any of the Asian countries.

Indonesia has simplified its procedures for foreign investment, but competition in that area, particularly from Japan and Europe, is brutal. A major project for the American Soybean Association is a feasibility review of setting up a transshipment facility in Asia, possibly in Indonesia, for bulk commodities. Basically, the question is whether creating another Amsterdam or Antwerp in Asia would enhance U.S. agricultural products.

India has reduced or eliminated a number of foreign investment restrictions since the introduction of its new industrial policy in July 1991. This liberalization has led to a surge in U.S. direct investment, which totaled approximately $1.14 billion by 1996. U.S. firms are beginning to understand the vast potential of this market with its estimated 200-300 million consumers, a vast pool of labor, and a developing financial system. Although import restrictions on some intermediary products have discouraged some U.S. companies from establishing themselves in this market, the United States continues to be the largest investor in India and its biggest trading partner. Despite slow economic growth and insufficient market transparency, the Indian economy has proved to be more stable and reliable than other Asian markets.

As Table 10-1 illustrates, the current Asian economic crisis has severely hampered U.S. agricultural export performance in the markets of the above mentioned Asian countries in 1997 and 1998, with the notable exception of India. The effects of the crisis on Asian demand for U.S. agricultural products could adversely alter the immediate prospects for investment in these countries. However, U.S. agribusinesses should not allow the current crisis to deter them from capturing the longer-term benefits of penetrating these markets.

Joint Ventures, FDI, and Training

Joint ventures and FDI are the most effective ways to strengthen the linkages between investment and trade. Investment provides access to markets. In fact, most large food manufacturers rely more heavily on FDI than on exports as their major strategy for accessing foreign markets. Unlike the situation a decade ago, the market strategy for export promotion today is the investment vehicle itself. In the late 1980s, U.S. food manufacturers held at least 10 percent equity in 720 food manufacturing affiliates overseas. That figure has grown exponentially, highlighting the importance of foreign affiliates. Foreign affiliates of U.S. food companies are more trade-oriented than their parent firms, exporting an average of 19 percent of their total production. In contrast, parent companies in the United States export only about 3.5 percent of their production.

In addition to providing investment, companies can offer technical assistance and training. Cargill, Incorporated, a model for many in the field, has an arm, Cargill Technical Services, that provides aid and technical assistance and is an excellent vehicle for finding investment opportunities overseas. For example, Cargill Technical Services had a U.S. Agency for International Development project in Uganda for three years, and within a year of the contract's expiration, the parent company bought a mill there. By offering technical assistance through U.S. programs and ensuring training as part of the investment package, corporations can help pay for market development costs. A company's service does not have to end at the doorstep of its facility; training increases returns and builds customer confidence, positioning a firm for countertrade and buyback opportunities.

Many Asian firms hope to enter the global marketplace as a joint venture partner, a direct exporter, or an affiliate of Western food or agricultural enterprises. But these firms cannot access the necessary financing unless they have a buyback formula. Indian banks, for example, often still require or favor trade financing or longer-term loans for domestic enterprises that have entered into a contract with foreign partners for a commitment to purchase a fixed quantity of the borrowing company's production.

TABLE 10-1
U.S. EXPORTS OF AGRICULTURAL, FISH, AND FORESTRY PRODUCTS TO SELECTED ASIAN COUNTRIES, FY (Oct.-Sept.) 1992-98 (US$THOU.)

Country	1992	1993	1994	1995	1996	1997	1998	% Change 1997-98
China	847,946	486,907	979,558	2,511,896	1,925,836	1,923,349	1,625,590	−15.5
Indonesia	371,766	348,636	428,181	741,426	943,173	803,394	565,806	−29.5
India	117,780	224,172	132,892	189,857	113,495	155,067	166,551	7.4
Malaysia	163,582	232,622	215,356	395,909	658,719	612,665	332,334	−45.7
Philippines	457,939	544,432	577,003	704,758	941,174	938,857	765,322	−18.5
Singapore	223,189	240,557	272,921	304,072	322,092	305,940	240,686	−21.3
Thailand	337,051	311,367	395,414	553,280	639,449	593,893	476,386	−19.8

Source: FAS, USDA.

Until 1997, the Reserve Bank of India required such buybacks as a provision for equity financing that originated overseas in transactions involving more than 51 percent foreign ownership. But in these arrangements, problems can arise in assigning a market value for a given amount of product for future delivery. This type of arrangement can often work against the supplier, despite the short-term benefit of immediate financing.

Nonetheless, U.S. companies would be well served to consider emerging markets beyond the traditional paradigm of another source of demand for products of U.S. origin. Companies should expand their strategies to look at these markets for domestic sales from a local subsidiary facility. U.S. agribusinesses should also consider opportunities to process a local product as an ingredient in the company's final product. Many countries in Asia are resource-rich, offering a quality product for direct marketing or ingredient processing. For value-added products, labor costs in Asia are low, and transport throughout Asia can be made cheaper by shipping smaller lots over shorter distances.

In addition, participating with nonagricultural companies in infrastructure and industrial development in Asian countries is worthwhile as a bridge to other markets. Logically, the United States should focus on its current account and trade bilaterally as well as multilaterally. But a longer-term view of the trade return on investment would justify piggybacking agribusiness and infrastructure investment. Moreover, the parent U.S. agribusiness company would increase intrasubsidiary trade by emphasizing the establishment of subsidiary operations in emerging markets. These subsidiaries could procure products of U.S. origin for further processing and sale in Asian and third-country markets.

Globally operated agribusinesses with an Asian presence have the advantages of direct marketing capability in regional markets and of enhancing U.S. exports. Once an economy reaches a certain threshold, as the current emerging markets have, American companies should treat them as part of the global marketplace. At present, the data show that a limited territorial definition for a market may overly restrict a company's total operations. Globalization is particularly relevant to the food, feed, and livestock industries.

CONCLUSIONS

Predicting the future is treacherous, but certain aspects are almost self-evident. Although in the short and medium terms, the current Asian crisis could stifle regional demand for U.S. products, the long-term prospects are excellent because of growing populations, expanding middle classes, liberalization, the effectiveness of WTO growth markets, and the increasing demand for the quality and variety of Western products. U.S. businesses generate significant secondary and tertiary effects in terms of classic economic development indices. Investment promotes economic and welfare benefits to the host country as well.

Significant changes will occur in operations and modalities of the U.S. food and agriculture industry. As the Asian region recovers from the current financial crisis and develops strong market economies, there will be great opportunities for U.S. food and agricultural interests not only in the sale of goods, but also in the development of a technical base with more efficient distribution, handling, storage, training, and extension. Examples of this are private-public sector cofinancing of port development and modernization projects, cold chains (refrigeration and distribution systems), and delivery systems.

Conceptually, then, U.S. corporations should think globally. Operationally, they should follow a few guidelines. First, companies should no longer think in terms of comparative advantage, but in terms of competitive advantage. That is, it is not so much the factors of production that determine whether a company is competitive, but how the firm's strategy and operations are organized. Second, the need for targeted, integrated production and marketing strategies must be taken into account. Finally, companies should build the strategic alliances that are so important in Asia. Following these guidelines takes considerable staying power. But staying power is required in these markets to benefit from their growth.

11

Opportunities for Grain Trade in Asian Markets

by Kevin D. Adams

*Vice President, Zen-Noh Grain Corporation and
Consolidated Grain and Barge Enterprises, Inc.*

Although Europe dominated the world economy and world agriculture in the 19th century, a new world economic order took shape in the 20th century as the U.S. economy matured and its resources were utilized. In grain and transportation, the industries in which Zen-Noh Grain Corporation and Consolidated Grain and Barge Enterprises are involved, another world economic swing is in progress, stemming from the strong influence of Asia. This chapter discusses grain trade in some of the Asian markets, with a focus on Japan's mature market. The rest of the Asian marketplace was just beginning to experience real economic growth before the onset of the Asian financial crisis. At that time, as the political climate stabilized, capital followed, seeking returns based on utilization of available resources. The results were spectacular economic growth and increased levels of disposable income, driving consumer demand and creating many opportunities for the grain and transportation industries. The Asian financial crisis has certainly created a setback in the economic growth of several of the Asian economies. This has resulted in a significant short-term reduction in consumer demand in some Asian countries. Over the longer term (three to five years), the outlook remains very promising as these economies are expected to recover and once again experience economic growth.

Zen-Noh and Consolidated Grain transport and merchandize grains and grain products such as soybean and corn gluten meal both in the United States and for export. In the grain industry, change is continual—changing consumers and products result in changing markets and economics. In the Asian marketplace, Zen-Noh and Consolidated Grain principally handle three types of grains—a generic-type grain, identity-preserved (IP) grains, and added-value grains. The challenges of marketing grains differ considerably in the Japanese marketplace and in the developing markets of East and Southeast Asia.

MARKETING GRAINS IN DIFFERENT ASIAN ECONOMIES

The Japanese Marketplace

As the Japanese market has matured, its imports of grain have leveled off. But Japan is increasingly focusing on IP and added-value grains, which provide incremental value to the processors. In economic and marketing terms, the players in the Japanese marketplace are trying to differentiate their products, as happens in mature markets. IP grains are varieties that are used for specific products such as tofu. With IP grains, the relationship between the exporter and the consumer, the company producing the product, is extremely important. The volume for this type of grain is small relative to total consumption, and Japanese trading houses are the key to accessing IP grain demands.

Grains that add incremental value trade in larger volumes and prove their value through test runs, either in feeding trials or processing facilities. These grains raise incremental value for the commercial consumer by increasing the value of the output of their processing or milling facilities.

The gatekeepers of the Japanese marketplace are the Japanese trading companies. Without their participation, it would be extremely difficult to access that market. As in most of Asia, relationships are important; once formed, they can endure for extended periods, sometimes even when economic factors would otherwise force change.

The opportunities for growth in the Japanese market for unfinished goods or raw materials such as grains are minimal. As trade barriers surrounding Japan are gradually eliminated, finished goods will continue to be imported, but at a slower pace because of Japan's cultural and historical reluctance to accept the intrusion of outsiders or the importation of products. Because its two shareholders are large Japanese companies, Zen-Noh and Consolidated Grain have learned to understand and work within this structure, which is significantly different from other Asian economies.

South Korea's Market

Although the South Korean marketplace is similar in some respects to Japan's, there are key differences. One is that trading companies in South Korea are not market gatekeepers to the extent that they are in Japan. Another is that the Korean grain market is still experiencing growth. Furthermore, the Korean consumers, i.e., the processors or feeders, are extremely price sensitive, demanding the lowest cost product when they buy a nutritional component regardless of the type of grain from which it comes. In contrast, processors and feeders in Japan do not vary feed ratios to take advantage of input price variations, but continue with their preferred blends.

Marketing in China and Southeast Asia

The development of China and Southeast Asia presents a variety of challenges. Unlike the case in Japan, the flow of business in these regions is dictated more by economic factors than by the relationship between exporter and consumer. The markets are young, and thus the growth of volume and total revenue is the overriding concern for most industries.

In China, the demand for feed grains and oilseeds to supply the rapidly growing livestock sector is outpacing the nation's ability to produce and transport the products. For example, its domestic demand for corn increased approximately 30 percent from 1993 to 1997, or by about 26 million metric tons. At the same time, China's domestic production has increased by only 13 million metric tons. That increase in demand is equivalent to 10 percent of the 1997 U.S. corn crop.

This trend is even more impressive for soybean meal, the other main ingredient of livestock feed. In 1993, China imported 8 thousand metric tons of soybean meal; in 1997, imports were projected to be 2.9 million metric tons—a 36,000 percent increase. During that four-year period, Chinese soybean production actually decreased 1 percent, and total oilseed production plateaued. Thus, as the livestock industry was growing dramatically, most of the protein used in formulating livestock feed was being imported.

To say that China has great potential is an understatement. China's economic growth is unprecedented, and many analysts consider it to be the single largest factor affecting growth and opportunity in Asia for agribusinesses, particularly in raw products. As world demand for feed grains increased during the 1970s and 1980s, the Soviet Union was a key factor. When the subsidized Soviet buying power disappeared, many concluded that total world demand had decreased. But a closer examination of total world demand for feed grains, excluding the Soviet Union and the former satellite countries, reveals that non-Soviet demand steadily increased during that period. Today, sound economic demand from the Asian countries has finally restored overall world demand to prior levels, and it will continue to increase because it is not subsidized demand. Rather, it is real economic demand driven by consumers' increased disposable income. The Asian crisis has impacted some Asian economies, and the decrease in consumer disposable income will be a negative factor for a short period of time (one to three years). By November 1998, most of those economies had already demonstrated signs of stabilization and a return to economic growth.

BUILDING BUSINESS RELATIONSHIPS

Relationships are very important in Asian business circles, opening doors and presenting business opportunities that do not exist otherwise. For this reason, most firms attempting to penetrate these markets find a business partner with local contacts, one who thoroughly understands the forces at work in the economies of the area. This strategy does not ensure success, but it provides the opportunity to compete. East and Southeast Asia have enormous potential for growth in agricultural trade, and the United States must compete with suppliers around the world such as South America, Australia, and India.

MANAGING RISK

Credit risk in Southeast Asia is a part of every transaction and substantially increases in international trade. Credit risk in countries like Japan, particularly when Japanese trading houses are used as an intermediary, has been essentially viewed as nonexistent. However, given the Asian crisis, this can no longer be taken for granted. But the same cannot be said for developing countries in Southeast Asia, and extreme caution must be used when pursuing direct business with small companies. In agricultural trade, the largest risk is that a customer will default on a contract. That is a significant problem because even companies that have confirmed irrevocable letters of credit in place cannot be protected from default without posted performance bonds, and Asian buyers often do not post them. The recent Asian financial crisis should serve as a reminder of the critical nature of this issue.

SUMMARY

As the Asian economies recover from the financial crisis, there will be substantial room for business growth for any company with sufficient capital. The selection of the right business partner is critical and may ultimately determine the venture's success. Worldwide grain and transportation industries are mature industries that will find new opportunities in the markets of Southeast Asia.

12

Rapid Growth in U.S. Export Markets for Poultry

by William F. Kuckuck

President, International Sales,
Tyson Foods, Inc.

At Tyson Foods, worldwide income growth is viewed as the driving force behind the demand for U.S. exports, particularly for food products. Don Tyson, Chairman of Tyson Foods, predicts that as incomes rise from the level of basic necessity, more food and certainly more protein will be consumed.

UNPRECEDENTED EXPORT GROWTH

Never before in the history of the poultry industry have U.S. producers focused so intently on sending products abroad. Between 1989 and 1993, poultry exports doubled in value, reaching $1 billion. More amazingly, they doubled again from 1993 to 1995. Export value and volume continued to increase during the next two years, although at a slower rate, reaching $2.5 billion in 1997. Experts are not predicting an end to this trend, particularly when the consumption of some of the developing nations is compared with that of the developed nations. Although the poor economic conditions in Asia have caused a drop in consumer spending, poultry continues to be in strong demand. Prices for imported poultry have necessarily declined, but volume should remain stable.

Since 1985, worldwide consumption of poultry has increased approximately 60 percent. In the same period, pork consumption has grown 30 percent, whereas beef consumption has remained relatively unchanged. To meet the growing demand for poultry, poultry products will be produced either within the consuming country or by countries that have a competitive advantage and the ability to export. Among the top 10 poultry exporting nations in the world, the United States has seen its market share grow from 30 percent in 1990 to almost 60 percent in 1997.

UNCERTAINTIES IN THE POULTRY EXPORT MARKET

Although the export of poultry may seem straightforward, numerous issues confront U.S. poultry exporters. One of the major concerns is the lack of market diversification. The industry ships a large volume of dark meat to Russia and exports many chicken parts (paws, wing tips, and other by-products) not consumed in core markets to Asia.

A second area of concern to the industry is trade credit or consumer credit. Payment is not assured in many U.S. export markets. This stems in part from the inexperience of some of the companies in the poultry industry, as well as from the inexperience of U.S. bankers in dealing with foreign bankers regarding terms of credit. This has led to a lack of trust between U.S. exporters and their customers, particularly in Southeast Asia where personal relationships and trust are key to long-term business success. The constant worry about whether to finance a transaction has resulted, to some degree, in a lack of goodwill between these nations and U.S. producers. In light of the Asian crisis, many U.S. exporters have grown more cautious than in past years and are no longer able to be as flexible on letter of credit terms. In addition, they are negotiating with U.S. banks more often and are watching receivables more closely.

Another issue for exporters relates to logistics. In most of the importing Asian countries, the infrastructure for perishable products is below U.S. standards and many Asian homes lack refrigeration, creating considerable concerns about food safety. The transport and delivery of fresh, wholesome products to the consumer is extremely important, but it can be difficult to find refrigerated equipment to deliver the products to supermarkets and stores. Further, the cold storage industry that is commonplace in the United States is absent from many Southeast Asia countries and scarcely exists in China.

When Tyson Foods began exporting to Asian markets, it faced relatively little competition. Now, however, there are major poultry exporters from South America, particularly Brazil. China and Thailand are key competitors of the United States in Asia, with Thailand particularly strong in the value-added poultry product field.

In addition, a looming issue is China's potential level of competition in Asian poultry markets. On the one hand, given the size of the Chinese population and the rate of growth of its domestic poultry consumption, some analysts predict that China's poultry producers may at best merely be able to keep up with the needs of their own consumers. On the other hand, others point to the fact that China is well positioned in Asian markets and has the technology and readily available labor to become a major poultry exporter. For example, China currently exports a large and fast growing volume of fresh poultry products to Japan.

THE IMPACT OF FAST FOOD ON ASIA

There has been phenomenal growth in Southeast Asia of the value-added side of the poultry business, which includes breaded breast products and nugget-type products that are sold in fast-food stores. Further, within the next 5 to 10 years, major U.S. fast-food restaurants and chains expect to expand in Asia by 200, 500, or 1,000 restaurants. This growth will have a significant impact on Southeast Asia, where it is already starting to change consumers' preferences. Many of the products that are sold in these restaurants are based on white meat, whereas Asians at present prefer dark meat. It will be interesting to see if preferences change in Asia as they have in the

United States, where the older generation preferred dark meat while today's generation prefers white meat. A similar reversal of preferences could occur in world markets.

Contributing to the growth of fast-food chains in Asia is a young population. In Southeast Asia, 34 percent of the population is under the age of 14. Thus, a greater number of Asians may soon be eating in fast-food restaurants, which could dramatically affect the growth of the poultry industry in world markets.

SUMMARY

Poultry exporters are currently enjoying a boon. Consumers around the world are buying high quality U.S. poultry products at affordable prices. The U.S. poultry industry must continue to give the world a good, wholesome product that is available where and when people want to buy it.

PART IV

VIEWS ON THE REGION'S FOOD AND AGRICULTURAL FUTURE

13

U.S.-Japan Agricultural Relations

by Kaoru Yoshimura

*Former Agricultural Counselor,
Embassy of Japan, Washington, D.C.*

T he United States has long been the leading agricultural supplier to Japan, and Japan has been the number one market for U.S. agricultural products. In 1996, Japan imported $43 billion worth of agricultural products, of which $16 billion (38 percent of total Japanese agricultural imports) came from the United States. In the same year, 20 percent of U.S. agricultural exports went to Japan, exceeding the value of U.S. agricultural exports to the entire European Union. In 1996, the United States supplied 61 percent of Japan's beef imports, 97 percent of its corn imports, 79 percent of its soybean imports, 53 percent of its wheat imports, and 87 percent of its tobacco imports. Japan was a market for 66 percent of U.S. red meat exports by value and 29 percent of U.S. coarse grain exports.

Agricultural trade between the United States and Japan is expanding. For example, after Japan began to import rice in accordance with the Uruguay Round agreement in 1994, the United States supplied 46 percent of Japan's rice imports in 1995 and 1996 and 50 percent in 1997. This new business was a significant change for the U.S. rice industry. Pork exports have also been increasing. Although U.S. pork producers showed little interest in exporting to Japan 10 years ago, in 1996, the United States surpassed Denmark, a traditional pork exporter, to become the second largest supplier to Japan. The reason for this growth is that Japanese consumers value the high quality of U.S. pork. The same situation exists for fresh and frozen vegetable exports such as broccoli and asparagus. California broccoli is readily available in Japanese supermarkets and even in conventional grocery stores. This situation could not have been imagined a decade ago.

PROSPECTS FOR U.S. EXPORTS

In future U.S. agricultural trade with Japan and Asia, the increase in populations and in income levels will be the major factors defining demand. Based on United Nations projections, the total Asian population will increase by 800 million by 2010 and by 1.5 billion by 2025. In contrast, the population of developed countries, including Japan, will increase by only 70 million by 2025, just one-twentieth of the total Asian population growth in the next 30 years. In terms of income, international organizations such as the World Bank estimate that annual real economic growth per capita in the decade beginning in 1992 will be 3.4 percent in South Asia and 5.9 percent in East Asia, rates that are much higher than those in other areas of the world. Clearly, there is enormous potential demand for agricultural products in Asia and a huge market for U.S. agriculture. However, Japan does not have the same prospects for population increase or high economic growth that exist in other Asian countries.

In terms of production, future agricultural productivity growth in Asian countries involves many uncertainties, including the amount that is invested in agriculture and in agricultural research. Although most Asian countries will attempt to enhance their agricultural sectors, it is difficult to satisfy increasing and changing demands that result from income growth, a problem that Japan faced during the past three decades.

The United States is in a strong position in agricultural trade with East and Southeast Asia, exemplified by the beef trade with Japan. In the 1996 Japanese fiscal year, the volume of Japan's beef imports from the United States surpassed those of Australia for the first time, and the United States became the leading foreign supplier in the Japanese beef market.

Because of the Japanese preference for sirloin and tenderloin, U.S. exports are directed toward these parts. Given its huge domestic beef market, the United States is able to export just sirloin and tenderloin to Japan and consume other parts within the United States. However, U.S. competitors in the international beef market cannot follow this trend because their domestic markets are smaller. Instead, they export certain parts to Japan and the others to the United States. But as the competition for the U.S. market becomes more severe, beef exports to the United States from competing countries may fail to grow at the previous rate, and those countries could lose their share in the Japanese beef market as well.

In other words, the United States can stably supply specific products in accordance with the needs of importing countries because of its enormous domestic demand. The food culture in East and Southeast Asia varies by country and area, and so do needs for agricultural products. Thus, the size and diversity of U.S. agriculture is a great advantage in Asian markets.

CONCLUSION

Although a large share of U.S. agricultural products already goes to the Japanese market, it is notable that agricultural trade between the United States and Japan has been increasing yearly. This key element will continue to shape the relationship of U.S. agricultural exporters as reliable suppliers and Japanese agricultural consumers as accountable customers. Next on the U.S. agenda probably will be to extend this type of relationship to all of East and Southeast Asia. This will involve many challenges, including the accession of some countries to the World Trade Organization and the continuing fallout from the Asian financial crisis that began in 1997. Nevertheless, Asian countries are eager to pursue this mutually beneficial relationship.

14

China's Food and Agricultural Development Prospects and Policies

by Wan Baouri

Vice Minister of Agriculture,
People's Republic of China

I n recent years, China's agriculture and food supply have become an issue of world concern. Some analysts believe that China will scarcely be able to feed its population in 20 or 30 years. There are several reasons that the world should be concerned about China's food supply and agricultural development:

- A population of 1.2 billion makes China a huge food-producing and food-consuming country.

- China is in a period of rapid economic growth, and its demand for food and other farm commodities is continuously expanding.

- Since reform and the open-door policy were introduced, China has intensified its agricultural contacts with the world.

- Declining world grain stocks and rising prices on the international market have worsened global food security in recent years.

CHINA'S CURRENT AGRICULTURAL STATE

Before turning to China's future food and agricultural development, the country's present agricultural status must be examined. China has 22 percent of the world's population and relatively limited land, a little more than 7 percent of the world's total arable land. These basic facts explain why food supply is always a fundamental issue in China's economic development and social stability.

Since the early 1980s when China launched its policy of reform and openness to the outside world, the nation's output of major farm commodi-

---

This chapter has been adapted from a presentation at the 1997 National Agricultural Forum in Des Moines, Iowa, and updated as of November 1998.

ties has increased by a large margin, and its living standards have dramatically improved. In 1996, total output of grain was over 480 million metric tons, meat output was 58 million metric tons, and production of fishery products was 28 million metric tons—gains of 57.4 percent, 520 percent, and 500 percent, respectively, compared with figures before the early 1980s. Further, China's per capita output has reached 394 kilograms (kg) of grain, 48 kg of meat, and 23 kg of fishery products, levels that equal or surpass the world average. The average Chinese has a daily intake of 2,727 calories, 70 grams of protein, and 52 grams of fat, among the highest levels compared with countries that have similar per capita gross national product (GNP) values.

With the country's basic subsistence problem solved in the mid-1980s, China's goals for its food and agricultural development have been to further boost grain output while diversifying food production to accommodate changing diets and to steadily improve the quality of life.

Based on the country's national economic development plan and the population's dietary habits, the future diet of the Chinese will include average caloric intake, high protein intake, and low fat intake. This will no doubt result in an increase in the share of animal-based food and the maintenance of the traditional pattern of plant-based food. Because of this changing diet, grains directly consumed by people will continuously decrease, and the use of feed grains will gradually increase. Given this consumption pattern and future population growth, China's grain demand for the next several decades is projected as follows: When the population approaches 1.3 billion in 2000, total grain demand will be around 500 million metric tons; when the population reaches 1.4 billion in 2010, demand will be about 550 million metric tons; and when the population peaks at 1.6 billion in 2030, demand will jump to about 640 million metric tons.

MEETING FUTURE FOOD DEMAND

Some specialists and scientists doubt that China will be able to improve living standards and diets because per capita output of grain is not expected to significantly increase. However, several factors indicate that China can accomplish this goal.

First, the current arable land utilization rate is not high, and there is substantial potential for increasing the unit yield with the help of science and technology. Second, although per capita output of grain may not greatly increase, prospects are good for diversifying food production by utilizing nonfarm land resources. Moreover, by promoting technical progress in livestock and fish farming and by improving the feed conversion rate, the ever increasing demand for feed grains can be eased. Third, the growing supply and consumption of meat, eggs, fishery products, and fruits and vegetables will gradually replace grain consumption. Fourth, with the introduction of social security reforms in areas such as health care and housing, urban families' investment horizons will expand, and the growth of incomes will exceed the growth of food consumption.

Can China, in the face of growing food demand, balance grain supply and demand early in the next century? The country faces many difficulties in realizing this goal: A huge population dependent on limited land resources; shortage of water; weak agricultural infrastructure; the small production scale of farming; and the fact that resource distribution under market economy conditions is not conducive to agricultural development.

In spite of such problems, China's future agricultural development holds great promise. Past experience shows that fulfilling future grain output targets is within the country's capability. For example, satisfying a demand of 640 million metric tons in 2030 will require less than 1 percent annual average growth in total grain production; over the past 47 years, the average grain output growth rate was 3.1 percent a year. Meeting this grain production target is economically and technically possible in China. Two-thirds of the cultivated land is average or low yielding, with output ranging from 3,000 kg/ha (hectare) to 5,000 kg/ha, which is about 50 percent less than the yield of high yielding land. Nevertheless, engineering and biotechnology can help improve this land to substantially raise unit yield. At present, the share of agricultural science and technology in boosting farm production is only 35 percent; it is expected to reach about 50 percent by the end of the century. In countries with developed agriculture, this share currently surpasses 60 percent.

Although China's agricultural science and technology development still lags, there are other potential avenues for agriculture growth. More than 20 million hectares of barren land are suitable for agriculture. This land will be reclaimed in a planned way to offset past land loss caused by occupation for nonfarm purposes and to stabilize the area of cultivated land. China may be limited in arable land, but it is rich in other resources such as grassland, hill land, barren land, and water areas, which are ideal for nongrain food production.

In addition, losses in grain production, distribution, and consumption are at least 10 percent at present. If China could reduce this loss to a reasonable degree, it might save 20 million metric tons of grain a year.

China's confidence in further developing food and agriculture stems not only from the country's vast potential, but also from the government's policy of making agriculture a top priority in national economic development. Since reform and the open-door policy were launched, China has formulated a series of fundamental policies that dovetail with market economy requirements and help to implement farmers' initiatives. All of these policies will greatly advance China's agricultural development. The painstaking efforts and determination by the Chinese government and the Chinese people will assure that future agricultural development targets will be met.

ACHIEVING SELF-SUFFICIENCY

To solve its food supply and demand problems, China has adopted a policy of self-sufficiency. Pursuing this basic policy does not preclude replenishing supplies from the international market when needed. However, grain is imported only to adjust stocks, balance regional differences, or offset yield declines in lean years. Under normal circumstances, China will maintain a self-sufficiency rate of no less than 95 percent and net grain imports of no more than 5 percent of total domestic consumption.

Why should China uphold such a policy? First, for a country of 1.2 billion people, a high degree of grain self-sufficiency is essential for economic development and social stability. Second, food production provides job opportunities for rural laborers. For the more than 400 million rural workers in China, developing agriculture is a major way to expand rural employment and farmers' incomes. Third, China's policy of self-sufficiency contributes to world food security. Annual food consumption in China is one-fifth of the global total. If China were to import large amounts of grains, not only would the world market find that demand difficult to meet, but also low income and food-deficit countries would suffer from tight world supplies. Therefore, solving China's food problems internally will help improve world food security and further stabilize international grain trade.

In the past 10 years or so, China's net grain imports were limited, less than 1 percent of total domestic grain production; during that period, China also exported grains. From 1992 to 1994, China's net grain exports averaged 13.2 million metric tons a year. China also exports high quality value-added food products. From 1985 to 1995, China's exports of poultry and livestock products for human consumption were valued at $75.6 billion and its imports of those products at $34 billion, thus making China a net food exporter. China is willing to establish stable food and farm commodity trade relationships with all countries on the basis of equality and mutual benefit.

MAJOR AGRICULTURAL POLICIES

The Chinese government will employ seven major policy measures to accelerate the stable development of agriculture, particularly grain production.

1. Deepen reforms and improve the market economy mechanism. For more than a decade, reform has directly resulted in rapid agricultural development; to achieve sustainable agricultural development in the future, these efforts will be deepened. Priorities include encouraging farmers to transfer their right to land use according to law and gradually expanding the scale of land management in areas where conditions permit. China intends to perfect socialized agricultural service systems, develop intermediary organizations linking farm households to markets, and establish commercialized enterprises connecting production, processing, and marketing to enhance the economic efficiency of agriculture. Further, China will reform the food distribution system, establish market-driven price mechanisms, and encourage open management. The government will improve its grain reserve and regulation function and strengthen the role of the minimum protection price and risk fund to buttress its macroeconomic control over the grain market.

2. Protect arable land in accordance with law and preserve the country's sown area. The occupation of farmland for nonfarm purposes must be strictly controlled through legislation. Barren land suitable for farm production must be reclaimed rationally, taking into account ecological and environmental protection concerns. Moreover, China must reform the traditional farming system, develop intercropping and multiple cropping, and increase the land's cropping index to ensure the dynamic balance of total arable land and to stabilize the cropped area on a long-term basis.

3. Implement a strategy of invigorating agriculture through science, technology, and education and by accelerating agricultural technical advancements. China's "Seed Project" is expected to raise the use of hybrid seed varieties in grain production by 95 percent by 2000. The agricultural technical extension and service networks will be improved at all levels, and advanced farming practices will be extended and popularized. Efforts will be made through research and development to overcome the technical limitations of grain production and other agricultural production. Technical training and education efforts that enhance farmers' understanding and use of science and technology in farm production will be strengthened.

4. Increase input efficiency and improve agricultural production conditions. China will readjust income distribution patterns and increase the share of financial and credit resources directed to agriculture. Policy measures will be adopted that enhance the efficient use of agricultural inputs and that encourage farmers to invest more in farm production. More resources will be channelled into agriculture from society as a whole. In the future, the government will invest mainly in agricultural infrastructure construction such as large- and medium-scale water conservancy works and in agricultural industry development such as chemical fertilizer plants. China will continue to improve low and average yielding land through integrated engineering and biological measures. The goal is to improve 14 million hectares of land in five years.

5. Develop and utilize nonfarm land resources to promote diversified food production. China will gradually establish a pattern of animal husbandry in line with China's resources, creating a forage-based livestock farming industry. Efforts will be made to develop cattle and sheep farming by utilizing crop residues (stalks and roughage) and at the same time to accelerate the production of compound feed and feed additives. There will be large-scale efforts to improve pastures, including reseeding to raise the pastures' livestock-holding capacity. In addition, work will intensify on developing and utilizing shallow sea water, coastal marshland, and inland water areas for aquaculture.

6. Control population growth and offer rational consumption guidance to the people. China will continue to implement a family planning policy to bring rapid population growth under control and to improve the quality of life. The government will encourage consumption habits on a scientific and thrifty basis and will oppose extravagance and waste. Moreover, China will restrict the production and consumption of liquors and wines derived largely from grain and develop industries that produce liquor using fruit or low percentages of grain.

7. *Protect natural resources and the environment and achieve sustainable agricultural development.* Large-scale water and soil conservancy activities will be carried out to address soil erosion problems in small watershed areas, prevent land and pastures from desertification and degradation, protect existing vegetation, continue a national afforestation campaign to increase forest coverage, and bring environmental pollution caused by industrialization under control through legal, administrative, and economic measures.

CONCLUSION

Over the past 10 years or so, China has taken major steps to open its agriculture to the world, and continuation of this open policy is an important measure in the successful development of this sector. A large amount of foreign funds has been absorbed to ease, to a certain extent, the shortage of domestic agricultural development funds. By 1995, China had used more than $10 billion of foreign financial resources to introduce advanced agricultural technology and equipment to accelerate the pace of agricultural modernization. China will actively develop international trade in farm commodities, which totaled $12.2 billion in imports and exports in 1995.

In general, however, agriculture has not been opened enough. Agriculture is a priority industry in the country; it is also a key industry supported by the government. In the future, China will follow commonly used international practices to further open the domestic market, to optimize the investment and trade environment, and to create more favorable conditions for agricultural-related economic, technical, and trade cooperation and exchanges with other countries. The United States, a country with a developed food and agricultural sector, is already an important farm commodity trading partner with China. China encourages U.S. agribusinesses to expand their investment in China's agricultural development. The Chinese government and the Ministry of Agriculture are ready to offer active coordination and positive support for cooperative measures that help achieve mutual development. At the threshold of the 21st century, a concerted effort should be made to promote Sino-American agricultural exchanges to contribute to food and agricultural development in a "borderless" world.

15

Australia's Strategy for Food and Agricultural Trade with East and Southeast Asia

by Paul Morris

*Minister-Counsellor, Agriculture and Resources,
Embassy of Australia, Washington, D.C.*

Despite the financial crisis in Asia that began in 1997, the long-term prospects for trade growth in the region remain favorable. Continued population expansion combined with a deficit of food production and prospects for a return to solid economic growth all bode well for future agricultural trade. Trade liberalization through multilateral agreements (World Trade Organization, WTO), regional agreements (Asia-Pacific Economic Cooperation, APEC), and unilateral efforts (such as those being encouraged in certain countries by the International Monetary Fund, IMF) are also leading to a more open environment that will be conducive to increased trade in the future. Even now, this region buys more Australian merchandise than the rest of the world combined, and trade to the region has held up remarkably well despite the downturn in certain economies. Nevertheless, breaking the barriers to trade in the Asian region will be one of the greatest challenges facing negotiators when the next round of multilateral negotiations commences in 1999.

This chapter provides an overview of Australia's strategies to increase trade in the region, focusing on those that address competitiveness in the medium to long term. The chapter does not discuss the details of the strategies being adopted to address the Asian financial crisis, but the Australian government has been active in contributing to IMF packages in Asia, providing credit insurance for exporters to South Korea and Indonesia, and in other ways such as aid donations.

Australia's medium- to long-term strategies to expand trade to Asia are based on three main premises. First, competitiveness begins at home. Selling to Asia requires a competitive domestic industry; therefore, domestic policy settings must be on target. Second, efforts to secure market access must be comprehensive, covering bilateral, regional, and multilateral approaches.

This chapter has been adapted from a presentation made in March 1997 and updated as of December 1998.

92

Third, markets do not develop on their own. The private sector and government can work together to develop markets and promote Australian businesses and exports in Asia.

AUSTRALIA'S TRADE WITH ASIA

The growth in Asia's share of Australia's exports has been remarkable. After accounting for only around one-third of Australian merchandise exports in the mid-1970s, the Asian region now accounts for more than one-half of these exports, with Japan alone accounting for 20 percent. Seven of Australia's top 10 markets are in Asia. The key growth markets for Australia have been South Korea, China, Taiwan, Hong Kong, and the Association of Southeast Asian Nations (ASEAN).

Asia is a vital market for Australian agricultural products. Two-thirds of all wheat, sugar, and beef exports, 50 percent of wool exports, and 90 percent of lobster exports go to Asia. For highly processed foods, Asia also dominates, accounting for over three-fourths of Australia's exports. While the recent difficulties in Asia are likely to cause some decline in export shares to the region, medium- to long-term prospects for increased trade remain favorable.

Because of the strength of Australian exports to Asia, it may seem that Asian markets are relatively open. Yet the opposite is true. Many barriers to trade with the Asian region exist that create problems for exporters from all countries. At the most aggregate level, the Organization for Economic Cooperation and Development (OECD) estimates of producer subsidy equivalents (PSEs) can be analyzed. In 1997, the estimated PSE for Japan was 69 percent, compared with an OECD average of 35 percent. The PSEs for the United States, Australia, and New Zealand were 16, 9, and 3 percent, respectively.

Tariff escalation in the region continues to be a major policy issue even though average tariffs have fallen. For example, although ASEAN has reduced applied tariffs, high levels of protection are being maintained for processed food.

Nontariff barriers in the region are also of concern. Examples of such barriers range from customs formalities (which can be a problem when they delay the delivery of fresh produce) through complex quota regimes. Sanitary and phytosanitary (SPS) barriers and packaging and labeling requirements that do not conform to international rules or that are unnecessary also create problems in several countries in the region.

TRADE POLICY OBJECTIVES

Australia's trade policy focuses on achieving improvements in the three areas mentioned above—competitiveness of its domestic industries, removing barriers in overseas markets, and promoting its products in Asia.

Domestic Policy Settings

The government has made significant improvements in Australia's domestic economy, and Australia's economic fundamentals are strong relative to other countries in the region. Apart from sound macroeconomic policies that have resulted in a 1997-98 budget surplus, low inflation (1.4 percent), and good gross domestic product growth, the government has applied industry policies that have heightened the performance of Australian industries to increase their exports and improve their prospects abroad. Competitiveness of domestic industries is determined by many factors, including a sound macroeconomic foundation and microeconomic reform in transport, public utilities, and shipping. But appropriate domestic policy settings, including increased access to Australia's markets, are of particular importance for at least three reasons.

First, Asian economic growth will be based on growth both in domestic consumption and in exports. The excellent growth prospects for the region are based to a large degree on strong export growth. Because a fair proportion of what Australia and the United States export to Asia is re-exported back to the respective country, domestic barriers can backfire and harm economic well-being. Second, limits on export growth in Asia created by barriers in other parts of the world will limit growth in domestic income and thus in domestic consumption. Growth estimates for food consumption in Asia by 2000 range from $160 billion upwards. While these estimates may have been reduced somewhat by recent events, this consumption growth depends on the income growth generated in part by exports. Again, barriers can backfire. Third, protected industries are less competitive and tend to be less export-oriented.

The Australian wine industry is a good example of the complementarity that can exist between imports and exports of a product. The industry decided some years ago that its market would be the world, and the more discerning wine drinkers of the world at that. In this, it has achieved spectacular success. In the past five years, Australian wine exports have increased 50 percent in volume and 100 percent in value.

However, over the same period, wine imports into Australia have increased 80 percent in volume, but the value of those imports has increased by less than 50 percent. The wine industry accepted lower priced wine imports for the appropriate end of the Australian market and exported high quality, high value products. The industry saw imports as an opportunity— not as a threat. Of course, Australian consumers also continue to get the best value wine in the world throughout the various market segments.

Removing Barriers to Overseas Markets

The second priority in Australia's trade policy settings is removing barriers to overseas markets. Once again, the government is focusing on three areas. First, Australia is pursuing better market access on a bilateral basis. In the past several years, Australia has signed a fruit market access agreement with the Philippines and has achieved access for fresh milk to

Hong Kong. Malaysia has also reduced its applied tariffs on wheat and liquid milk to zero; the Philippines has replaced its minimum access volume for beef with a declining tariff and opened up sugar access; and Thailand has reduced tariffs on a number of dairy products. Australia has also achieved concessions from Taiwan on wool, beef, and fruit linked to the accession of Taiwan to the WTO. The United States has recently had considerable success in achieving concessions from Taiwan linked to accession.

In 1996, Australia established the Market Development Task Force to give focus to bilateral trade efforts. The task force concentrates on a number of priority markets, including 11 in the Asian region—China, Hong Kong, India, Indonesia, Japan, Malaysia, Singapore, South Korea, Taiwan, Thailand, and Vietnam. For each of these markets, Australia has established specific sectoral priorities to achieve over the next two years, as delineated in the Trade Outcomes and Objectives Statements released in February 1997 and March 1998.

Second, the government is committed to expanding trade liberalization on a regional basis. It is committed to the principle of open regionalism and the exploration of new trade opportunities within that framework. At the center of this is APEC. The establishment of individual action plans for APEC countries has moved Australia toward freer trade in the region. These plans are a good beginning and confirm that APEC economies are on a clear path to liberalization.

Third, the Australian government has been engaged in strengthening the international trading system and in pressing members of the WTO for further trade liberalization on a global basis. A new round of agriculture negotiations commences at the end of 1999, which will provide an important opportunity to achieve further trade liberalization throughout the world, including the Asian region. Australia is keen to see these negotiations conducted in an expeditious manner and anticipates substantial reforms to be made in market access, export subsidies, and domestic support measures.

The gains that such liberalization can bring are clear. The export growth that both Australia and the United States have achieved is in no small part due to trade liberalization, both global and regional. Australian exports have been growing rapidly in recent years and reached a record of more than A$110 billion in 1997-98, despite the Asian crisis. This export growth has coincided with increased trade liberalization around the world, including the completion of the Uruguay Round, the establishment of APEC, and the growing recognition of the benefits derived from unilateral liberalization. It has been estimated that by the time the Uruguay Round reforms are completed for all sectors, the gains in income to Australia will be around A$5 billion per year.

Leading up to the 1999 negotiations, monitoring, negotiating, and, when necessary, use of dispute settlement procedures must be used to ensure that countries live up to their Uruguay Round obligations. Only then can the gains that were foreshadowed in the agreements be realized.

Opportunities for further reform also need to be embraced. For example, the applications by several Asian countries for accession to the WTO represent an important opportunity. A large number of countries are currently negotiating for membership in the WTO, including, in Asia, Cambodia, China, Nepal, Taiwan, and Vietnam. It is important to bring these countries on board so that they can be subject to the same disciplines as current WTO members to move toward a freer trade environment.

Promoting Australian Goods in Asia

On the final broad area of trade policy strategy, the government is concerned about utilizing its trade promotion and export assistance resources more effectively. Australia's "Supermarket to Asia" strategy is a central part of trade policy. The Supermarket to Asia Council was established in 1996 to provide leadership and drive to achieve success in Asian export markets. In particular, the council's mission is to remove export barriers, develop a much more aggressive export culture, and promote the benefits of Australian agrifood products in Asian markets. The focus has been on a quality food marketing and promotion program and opportunities online and in electronic commerce.

Five government ministers, including the Prime Minister, are represented on the council, as well as 11 private sector leaders. The council is a facilitation body whose primary role is to provide the strategic direction and priority setting for the agrifood industry, with the aim of increasing the number of successful food exporters to Asia.

The Council is developing new export opportunities by identifying barriers to trade throughout the value-added chain, marrying offshore opportunities to domestic capacity, and providing a liaison with food industry representatives and government at all levels. The council does this in conjunction with private sector working groups established under it. The government also provides support to small- and medium-scale enterprises through Export Market Development Grants as well as through specific industry programs.

CONCLUSION

Australia is adopting similar strategies throughout the world to ensure that Australian exports are not dependent on a limited number of markets and to provide a range of opportunities for exporters. Many of the areas in which Australia will be working are also areas of interest to the United States. Attempts to open markets through bilateral, regional, and multilateral efforts will be beneficial to all countries. The Australian government appreciates the U.S. leadership in the trade negotiations on agriculture, and it will continue to support U.S. efforts to achieve a freer world trading environment. Through these efforts, the growth forecasts for Asia can be realized, which will only benefit trading nations such as Australia and the United States.

16

The Indonesian Market for U.S. Agricultural Exports

by Edward E. Masters

President,
United States-Indonesia Society

East Asia's rapid economic growth until 1997 was not a miracle. A miracle would imply divine intervention. It was the result of tough decisions made by talented people against occasionally strong domestic opposition. Because they persevered, dramatic changes occurred in an area of increasing importance to the United States.

The World Bank reports that if pre-1997 economic growth trends had continued, however unlikely this might be, by 2020 the five largest economies in the world, measured by gross domestic product (GDP), would have been members of the Asia-Pacific Economic Cooperation (APEC) forum: China, India, Indonesia, Japan, and the United States. These countries in addition to Germany and South Korea (whether unified with the North) would have constituted the G-7 (the world's seven largest economies) by 2020. The finance ministers of the G-7 meet periodically to recommend solutions to the world's financial problems. Under this scenario, four current members, Canada, France, Italy, and the United Kingdom, would no longer be members of the G-7 by 2020 not because of declining economies, but because they would have lost ground relative to the other countries and would be replaced by Asian nations.

The financial crisis that began in 1997 has completely changed this picture. Indonesia is now in severe recession. The economy is expected to contract by approximately 15 percent. However, the country continues to have economic potential. It will recover and will again become a significant market for U.S. exports, including agricultural commodities.

CHANGING EATING HABITS BENEFIT U.S. EXPORTS

The agricultural trade relationship between the United States and the Association of Southeast Asian Nations (ASEAN) was, in general, good until late 1997. The ASEAN area—which includes the original five members (Indonesia, Malaysia, the Philippines, Singapore, and Thailand), the later addition of Brunei, Burma, Laos, and Vietnam, and the eventual accession of Cambodia—will have 500 million people before the end of the century. It is a growing market for U.S. produce. The U.S. Department of Agriculture

(USDA) estimates that U.S. exports to the ASEAN-6 (excluding Burma, Laos, and Vietnam) totaled around $3 billion per year during the first half of the 1990s. That is not a huge amount by global standards, but it is significant in certain sectors. It is interesting that one of the fastest growing U.S. exports to ASEAN before the financial crisis was fruit—Washington State apples, California grapes, and California and Florida oranges.

Eating patterns have shifted dramatically in the region. In Jakarta in the 1960s, bread was unavailable. Expatriates imported wheat flour and baked bread at home. In the 1970s, there were a few bakeries, and now there are many. Instead of eating rice three times a day, Indonesians are consuming wheat products at least once a day. This dramatic change in eating habits benefits the United States because it is an important supplier of wheat.

Cotton has been the largest commodity among U.S. agricultural exports to the ASEAN area. U.S. cotton is exported primarily to Indonesia and Thailand because of the reinvigoration of their boutique industries and the export of batik cloth and garments. U.S. exports of cotton to Indonesia peaked at $345 million in FY1995, then fell as a result of the financial situation to $230.8 million in FY1997 and to $156 million from January to August 1998.

According to USDA, the value of U.S. exports of agricultural, fish, and forestry products to Indonesia in 1997 was $803.3 million, a significant amount for that country. The value of bulk agricultural commodities alone was $489.9 million in 1997, of which $240.7 million was cotton and $197.8 million was soybeans. The value of intermediate products such as flour and various oils and meals was $156.8 million in 1997. In looking at figures for FY1998 until August, it is clear that U.S. exports have stumbled: Bulk agricultural commodities decreased 18.4 percent year on year (YoY); intermediate agricultural products declined 54.1 percent YoY; and consumer-oriented agricultural commodities fell 62.2 percent YoY. Few U.S. agricultural exports to Indonesia showed positive growth during FY1998 to August; however, rice, wheat, poultry, and planting seeds posted gains because of the prolonged drought and subsequent shortages of these commodities in the local market.

Two U.S. groups, the wheat growers and Washington State apple growers, have been particularly successful in promoting their products in Indonesia. The Washington State Apple Growers Association is a highly effective marketing organization. Although apples from New Zealand, Australia, and Chile are also on the market in Indonesia, the Indonesians—at least until the recent financial crisis—would buy an apple from Washington State even if it cost more.

PROTECTIONIST PRESSURES AND THE ASIAN CRISIS

Even before the full impact of the financial crisis hit, there were warning signs of increasing attention to inspection, consumer protection, and nontariff barriers on imported fruit. One article in an Indonesian business magazine commented: "The issue of imported fruit has gone far beyond the bounds of an economic matter and has entered the rarefied air of problems which touch on nationalism and pride. The influx of Navel and Valencia oranges from the United States and Australia, Delicious apples from Washington State, and Durian from Thailand have stirred a controversy. . . ." The climax of the article was as follows: "To date, Indonesia has no enforceable regulations regarding standards of quality necessary for imported fruit. Most observers of the situation believe that only through the establishment of such standards can Indonesia be able to protect not only its growers, but also its consumers from excessive use of pesticides. It is no secret that the country often becomes a dumping ground for products that could not be marketed in countries where there are more stringent rules."

The success of U.S. agricultural commodity exports to Indonesia in the coming years will largely depend on how quickly that country recovers from its worst economic recession in three decades. It is foreseeable that protectionist pressures in the coming years will be manifest in new ways as Indonesia imposes stricter management and promotion of domestic production and attempts to preserve much needed foreign exchange reserves. The dramatic drop in per capita income from $1,200 in 1997 to an estimated $450 by mid-1998 will also make imported consumer-oriented agricultural commodities prohibitively expensive for most Indonesians.

PART V

THE SPECIAL CASE OF CHINA AND ITS FUTURE DEVELOPMENT

17

China's Weak Banking System

by Nicholas R. Lardy

Senior Fellow, Foreign Policy Studies,
The Brookings Institution

Banking is the weak link in China's economic reforms. The core purpose of reform is to improve the efficiency with which capital is allocated. Yet there is little evidence that China's major banks have seriously begun to develop either the authority or the capability to allocate capital more rationally. The major banks remain state owned, and they are utilized by China's political authorities to fund priority state projects and, equally important, to underwrite the continued existence of many inefficient, money-losing, state-owned manufacturing and commercial enterprises.

As a result, China's financial system is extremely fragile. The state-owned banks, which account for virtually all bank assets, are woefully undercapitalized, and the reserves they have set aside for nonperforming loans are best described as minuscule. China's banks are only marginally profitable in the best of times; when inflation rises, they are hugely unprofitable.

FEATURES OF THE BANKING SYSTEM

Three unusual features characterize China's banking system. First, although China's banks rely almost entirely on savings deposits made by the public as the ultimate source of their funds, the banks lend almost exclusively

---

This chapter has been adapted from a presentation at the Hearing on Recent Developments in Banking and Finance in the People's Republic of China, Hong Kong, and Taiwan, Committee on Banking and Financial Services, U.S. House of Representatives, March 20, 1996, and updated as of November 1998.

to state manufacturing and commercial enterprises. There is basically no consumer credit in China. The state sector absorbs more than three-fourths of all loans by financial institutions, leaving the small remainder for the more dynamic, and now larger, nonstate portion of the economy. Thus, the banking system transfers funds from the public to the state.

Second, China's banks operate in a highly unusual interest rate environment. Because of the weak financial position of their major customers, banks are forced to extend loans at interest rates that are frequently far below the rate of inflation. The resulting negative real interest rate assures excess demand for loans and necessitates bureaucratic allocation of the available loan funds. However, to continue to retain and attract funds from the public during inflationary periods, the states banks are forced to raise the interest rates they pay to savers, particularly on longer-term certificates of deposit.

The net result is that during two periods of high inflation, with peaks in 1989 and 1994, China's major banks operated with negative interest rate spreads. That is, the amount they charged on loans was less than the amount they paid to depositors. The capital of the banks was subject to rapid erosion during both of these episodes.

Third, bank loans have grown extraordinarily rapidly since reform began, and an apparently large, but unknown, portion of these loans is nonperforming. The total loans outstanding of all financial institutions in China expanded from under ¥(yuan)200 billion in 1978, when reform began, to more than ¥5 trillion at the end of 1995. Loans outstanding at the outset of reform were about one-half of that year's gross domestic product. In 1996, the portfolio of loans outstanding was equal to 90 percent of GDP.

Most of the increased lending has gone to state enterprises. But the share of these enterprises that are losing money, and thus unable to amortize their debt, has expanded rapidly, reaching 44 percent in 1995. The state has directed an ever expanding flow of bank lending to these firms as an alternative to industrial restructuring, plant closures, and layoffs. The soft budget constraint has allowed inefficient enterprises to continue to operate and even, in many cases, to expand.

While such a strategy has obvious short-term political benefits, the long term economic consequences for the banking system have been adverse. China's banking authorities have conducted no comprehensive survey of the quality of bank assets. Thus, any estimate of the extent of nonperforming loans is subject to considerable uncertainty. But several authoritative Chinese sources have suggested that as much as one-third of the outstanding loans of banks and other financial institutions are nonperforming. Even if one assumes both that banks discontinue extending loans to bad credit risks immediately and that banks ultimately recover as much as one-half of their existing nonperforming loans from the proceeds of the liquidation of enterprises unable to amortize their debt, total financial losses would be 15 percent of gross national product and more than three times bank capital.

Thus, the costs (relative to the size of the economy) of recapitalizing China's banking system might dwarf the costs of dealing with the savings and loan crisis in the United States and the costs of dealing with the failures of banking institutions in both Japan and Mexico. The costs of the savings and loan debacle in the United States were about 2 percent of GDP. The estimated cost of dealing with the nonperforming loans of Mexican banks ranged from 5.7 percent to as much as 10 percent of Mexico's GDP. In Japan, the Ministry of Finance placed unrecoverable bank loans in 1995 at ¥18.3 trillion, about 4 percent of GDP, but Western estimates are higher than this official estimate.

THE OUTLOOK FOR CHINA

What are the implications of this analysis for China? First, recapitalizing the banking system and transforming it to operate on commercial principles so that only the more efficient enterprises have access to bank credit will be a long and costly process. It most likely will entail a dramatic increase in the stock of public debt outstanding and a period of slower economic growth. However, recapitalizing the banking system cannot begin in earnest until the state addresses the problem of inefficient, money-losing, state-owned enterprises. In short, it is not rational to begin addressing the problem of the accumulated stock of nonperforming loans until the annual flow of new nonperforming loans is stanched. Thus, the ultimate cost of rebuilding the fragile banking system depends largely on how much longer industrialization is delayed.

Second, China cannot realistically hope to achieve full convertibility of its currency on capital account until it strengthens its banking system financially. The present system is viable only as long as the public continues to increase its savings deposits in the banking system. To date, the state has accomplished this by a combination of two policies. First, banks have provided some insulation from the effects of inflation by indexing interest rates on longer-term certificates of deposit during periods of inflation. This has provided an important incentive for saving. In addition, and perhaps more important, the state has restricted the menu of financial assets available to savers. Full convertibility would allow the public to freely convert its domestic currency savings into foreign currency and then into financial assets held abroad. This process would quickly reveal the insolvency of the Chinese banking system. Thus, China's goal of achieving full convertibility prior to 2000 would appear to be unrealistic.

Finally, the costs of not undertaking the reforms suggested above are even greater. Ultimately, failing to transform the banking system to operate on commercial principles and simultaneously imposing a hard budget constraint on state-owned enterprises will mean the failure of China's economic reform. Without these reforms, capital will continue to be allocated inefficiently, ultimately dragging down the growth of the economy.

CONSEQUENCES FOR THE UNITED STATES

What are the implications of this analysis for the United States? First, China is unlikely to agree to a World Trade Organization (WTO) accession that requires it to quickly subject its inefficient state-owned industries to the full force of international competition. Such competition would result in widespread closures of enterprises and could precipitate a banking crisis. If the international community wants China to accede to the WTO and thus ultimately be subject to its disciplines, the United States and other industrialized countries will have to allow China to phase out its protection of a few sensitive industries over a period of several years. The phaseout period will have to be long enough to allow the Chinese government to deal with the problem of displaced workers.

Second, the efforts of the U.S. Department of the Treasury and the U.S. Trade Representative to persuade China to fully open its market to U.S. banks are not likely to be successful, at least in the short term. Because state banks have huge inventories of nonperforming loans, they would be unable to compete with foreign banks. Quite simply, in a liberalized financial environment, foreign banks would quickly run Chinese banks out of business. Nonetheless, U.S. negotiators should press for greater access to China's financial services market because competition from U.S. and other foreign banks could provide an important stimulus for banking reform in China. However, U.S. expectations in this area must be shaped by an adequate understanding of the current vulnerabilities of the Chinese banking system.

Third, under present circumstances, the Board of Governors of the Federal Reserve System and other relevant U.S. authorities should not approve the pending requests by China's largest state-owned banks to open branches in the United States. At a minimum, these banks fall far short of meeting U.S. required capital adequacy standards. Moreover, it appears that China's Central Bank does not effectively exercise prudential supervision of state-owned banks, even within China. Thus, China fails to meet the test of subjecting its banks to comprehensive regulation on a consolidated basis, a key criteria laid down by the Foreign Bank Supervision Enhancement Act of 1991 for licensing foreign banks to operate in the United States. The applications of Chinese banks should not be approved until both of these criteria are met.

In fact, applications by the Agricultural Bank of China, the China Construction Bank, and the Industrial and Commercial Bank for branch offices have been withdrawn. Instead, the Federal Reserve Board approved representative offices for each of the three banks. Since representative offices are limited to general marketing and promotional activities and are not allowed to conduct banking business, the criteria for approval of representative offices are far less stringent than those for branches. The branch office application by the Bank of China for its fourth U.S. branch office is still pending as of November 1998.

18

Moving Toward a Rules-Based
Financial System in China

by Douglas A. Scott

*Former International Monetary Fund
Resident Representative in China*

T o preface this discussion of China's modernization of its banking system, two observations must be made. First, for its reforms to be successful over a sustained period, China will have to move increasingly toward a rules-based financial system. This is frequently referred to as the rule of law, but it must also include many of the private or association rules of accounting, audit, and financial transactions and their settlement that exist throughout the Western economic system. Legally enforceable rules designed to protect the rights of private property and of people to buy, hold, and sell property are the foundation of modern economic systems. This is not the case in China, but it is the direction in which China's reform is and must continue moving.

Second, it is important to understand the background of those who work in Chinese institutions. People 38 years old or older most likely completed their university education by or before the mid-1980s. This means that they were educated in a university that had been reopened for less than 10 years, after having been closed for the entire decade of the cultural revolution. This point is significant because observers often refer to the gradual approach to economic reform in China without necessarily recognizing that a large part of Chinese society—those engaged in designing and implementing economic reforms—must learn about international economic arrangements and the economic systems and institutions that prevail in other countries. Such knowledge was not part of their education, and it is only beginning to filter into economics and law courses taught in major Chinese universities.

This chapter offers two propositions. The first is that trade and investment in agriculture will not prosper in China in the absence of macroeconomic stability. The second is that sound and competitive financial institutions are indispensable for commodity market development and macroeconomic stability.

MACROECONOMIC INSTABILITY

An important lesson from China's inflation of 1993 and 1994 is that neither trade nor investment in agriculture can prosper during periods of macroeconomic instability. In 1992, Chinese leaders expressed great confidence that inflation would not reemerge because China had learned its lesson from the inflation of 1988 and the disturbances later that year and in 1989. But the reality was that by early 1993, credit and financial markets were exhibiting disorderly conditions, and by the end of 1993 serious inflation had emerged.

The causes are now fairly well understood. Many stemmed from Chinese leader Deng Xiaoping's trip to the south early in 1992, during which he cajoled the people (and, by implication, the party elders) to accelerate economic reform and development. His famous series of speeches were so controversial at the time that it took several months before the Politburo allowed them to be published in the national press. Deng recognized that reform without growth was not going to be successful, as was the case in the Soviet Union in 1991. The result was a surge in investment by state-owned units that persevered from mid-1992 until late 1994; at times, the rate of growth of fixed asset investment was 70 percent over the previous year. This was the economic engine that ultimately reignited inflation in 1993-94.

An important manifestation of macroeconomic instability was the disorderly conditions in China's foreign exchange system. Early in 1993, the official exchange rate for the ¥ (yuan) was 5.8 per one U.S. dollar, whereas the market rate had depreciated to nearly ¥11 per one dollar. Sometimes transactions could not be conducted even at the more depreciated rate. Business people had to travel the country to find a counterpart for an individual foreign exchange transaction. "Ponzi" schemes proliferated. In addition to Deng's speeches urging acceleration of reforms and the subsequent robust fixed asset investment by state enterprises, the lack of effective mechanisms for macroeconomic regulation and control made inflation almost inevitable. China was still gripped by the dying convulsions of the planning system as the basis for macroeconomic control. Throughout the country, disregard for regulations, particularly those of the central authority, was widespread. This directly contributed to weak implementation of credit policy, taxation, government expenditure controls, and investment control.

Urban land reform, introduced in 1992, was a major contributor to the fever of speculation. The well-designed reform of the right to use land and the right to lease the use of land created, for the first time, a value for land and a mechanism of transferability. But it also laid the foundation for considerable land speculation and for much of the infrastructure and commercial rebirth now taking place, for example, in Shanghai. Without reform of the right to lease land, development in Shanghai today would look quite different.

Inflation and instability had consequences for China's agricultural policy. Inflation emerged in 1993 most conspicuously in urban areas in prices of consumer and investment goods. In rural areas, inflation was less pronounced until early 1994 when speculation in grains arose in part because of rumors that government food grain procurement prices would increase. This speculation was caused primarily by the government grain bureaus, which were responsible for managing the buffer stocks in the system. China also experienced a downturn in grain production in 1994, especially in Guangdong and neighboring provinces. The authorities were concerned that rising grain prices would reinforce other forces, causing inflation.

ACHIEVING GRAIN SELF-SUFFICIENCY

The food grain policy response was to introduce the "governor responsibility system." This system effectively steered the country back toward provincial, and lower level, grain self-sufficiency. Governors of provinces (and, through them, lower level authorities) were made responsible for grain supply and demand, balancing local production, slowing the alienation of land for nonagricultural purposes, and maintaining price stability or avoiding undue price increases. The governor responsibility system intensified border controls on the movement of grain from one province to another, except for movement through official trade channels.

Given the historical record of China since 1949, achieving food grain self-sufficiency in the first five years of economic reform was a major accomplishment. Reaching this goal was the result of dismantling the commune-based production brigades, introducing the household responsibility system, and developing rural markets. Fundamentally, the governor responsibility system was a natural administrative reaction to the sharp rise in grain prices and inflation, and it was a step back toward the earlier system of controls.

The issue for world agricultural markets is important. Will China continue to hold to a policy of grain self-sufficiency because of the importance of stable grain markets for national stability? Or will China move toward a more open system—under which Chinese agriculture specializes in activities that have the greatest economic advantage—and develop domestic markets for agricultural trade (including grain imports), integrating the nation more closely into international trade? The instability of 1993 and 1994 showed that China, at least at that stage, was not ready to move toward integration with, and dependence on, international markets.

There is also a political dimension to this issue that is a real consideration for China. From a Chinese perspective, China's interaction with the international community during the past 150 years has not always been favorable. To what extent do today's leaders want to put China's food security at the risk of the vagaries of the international market, including the recourse by some countries of trade restrictions or embargoes?

REFORMING CHINA'S FINANCIAL INSTITUTIONS

The second proposition is that sound and competitive financial institutions within China are indispensable for market development and macroeconomic stability. The recent acute problems in banking and other financial institutions in Thailand, Indonesia, and South Korea illustrate this proposition. China's response to the Asian financial crisis has been to carefully assess the implications in light of known weaknesses in its own large state banks and to formulate a bold program of bank reform, including recapitalization, in conjunction with reforming or closing many loss-making enterprises that are heavily indebted to banks.

Since 1993, China has made considerable progress in reforming its financial institutions and systems. But it still has a long way to go. Perhaps the greatest progress, in addition to the program noted above, has been in moving from the chaotic currency markets of 1993 to the convertibility of the currency in all current transactions. This transformation of China's foreign exchange system was remarkably speedy given the complexities and disorderly conditions prevailing in 1993.

Since 1993, the People's Bank of China, once a department of the State Council with primary responsibility for managing the planned and un-planned distribution of credit, has been transformed into the much more modern Central Bank of China and is working toward the effective use of modern indirect instruments of monetary policy.[1] This transformation accelerated with the Central Bank Law, which was developed in 1993 and adopted by the People's Congress in 1995. Since the beginning of economic reform in 1978, the Central Committee's most important economic action was probably the decision in November 1993 on the principles of the socialist market economy. The principles of this decision on monetary policy and the financial system were developed concurrently with the Central Bank Law. There are many parallels concerning the shift from credit planning to a market-oriented monetary policy and establishing a rules-based financial system in law and the decision of the Central Committee of November 1993.

For example, the Central Committee established that a branch of the Central Bank of China is indeed merely an agency of the head office and not an independent unit. This controversial issue was further clarified by the Central Bank Law and explicitly provided for in the Commercial Banking Law of 1995. These points demonstrate that China is in the process of adopting rules that U.S. and international business regard as normal. Although China is still in an early stage in, for example, developing property rights and the rule of law, it has made considerable progress in establishing a modern central bank

China has also begun to develop modern financial markets. It has interbank markets in local currency and in foreign exchange, and it has instituted rules, including rules for settlement of transactions and for non-observance of settlements. In addition, China is experimenting with the foundation of national rules and their counterparts for commodity markets. Thus, even though China, its laws, rules, and institutions, does not yet look like the typical market-based economic system, it is moving in the right direction.

Another fundamental aspect of moving toward a rules-based financial system is the adoption of modern accounting standards and their implementation in modern accounting systems. These steps must be supplemented by effective audit procedures—internal and external—for the banks. These are the bases of modern prudential supervision. Indeed, early in 1998, the State Council did decide that China would follow modern international accounting standards. Such standards are the foundation of rules-based banking and, ultimately, of transparency in banking. China understands the importance of prudential standards, but finds it difficult to accept the underlying concept of accounting standards and asset valuation. If China were to accept international financial practices on asset valuation, its large state commercial banks would face significant problems in reinterpreting their balance sheets. Transitional arrangements will be necessary to phase in new accounting standards and to meet international capital adequacy rules.

China will undoubtedly continue its move toward a modern rules-based financial system, but in the typical Chinese way, it will take time (in part reflecting the need to train sufficient numbers of professional staff in all relevant institutions), and it will be pragmatic. China wants its banks to participate as branches in foreign countries, particularly the countries of the G-10, but it recognizes the difficulties ahead. This will require a sound system of supervision over solvent banking institutions. The United States should be encouraged by the Chinese government's acknowledgment of the importance of accelerating reform of state-owned enterprises. Further, in 1998, the government approved a large bond issue to initiate bank recapitalization and clear balance sheets of bad loans. This process should facilitate adoption of sound accounting practices and resolution of important state enterprise problems in addition to strengthening the financial position of banks.

THE STEPS AHEAD

To enable China's financial system to serve its role and to develop competitive markets, the introduction of modern accounting systems, audit, and asset valuation is of fundamental importance. These are also major steps toward a system of prudential supervision. Second, a modern national payment system is needed. This has been under development since the early 1990s, and it will probably be several more years before China's automated payment system is functioning on a national scale. It is a tribute to Chinese ingenuity that China was able to put in place the technology for interbank and foreign exchange markets in the absence of a sophisticated national payment system.

In the rural area, China must overcome the weaknesses of the rural credit cooperative system, the agriculture bank, and even the new agricultural development bank. From a macroeconomic point of view, seasonal crop finance must be seasonal, which it has not been because of poor repayment experience. It has become part of the working capital that is loaned to the countryside, villages, and cities at the county level. China must develop a viable rural financial system to better serve the needs of agricultural producers and primary level marketers. This infrastructure is essential for China to build reasonably efficient national markets for trade in agricultural commodities. Finally, China probably will not accept a high degree of integration in international markets until it is confident that it is on the correct path in developing its internal agricultural markets.

The elevation of Executive Vice Premier Zhu Rongji to Premier of the State Council in 1998 signals the importance that party and government leaders attach to strengthening the process of economic reform. Recent policy pronouncements, especially concerning banks, loss-making state-owned enterprises, and government entities, reaffirm the direction and the speed of reform set forth by the Central Committee in 1993. This steadfastness of purpose and consistency are encouraging signs of strength in China's overall process of economic reform and opening to the international economic system.

NOTE

1. A central aspect of this transformation was to shift from a credit policy characteristic of planning systems to a monetary policy that enables market mechanisms to determine interest rates for the key policy targets (bank reserves).

19

Targeting Agricultural Prospects in Asia: Ranking China

by Erland Heginbotham

*Former Chief, China Agricultural Strategy Project,
Institute for Global Chinese Affairs
University of Maryland-College Park*

Gauging export prospects in East and Southeast Asia is exceptionally important because the region accounts for more than 40 percent of U.S. agricultural exports by value. Two prevailing characteristics deserve emphasis. First, Japan alone accounts for one-half of all U.S. agricultural exports to Asia. Second, more than one-half of U.S. agricultural exports to the leading markets in East Asia are processed foods—primarily meat, fish, and soybean oil.

In 1994, four secondary Asian markets—South Korea, Taiwan, the five key Southeast Asian countries as a group (Indonesia, Malaysia, the Philippines, Singapore, and Thailand), and China—each took 10 to 12 percent of the global U.S. agricultural exports by value (Table 19-1). With the accession

TABLE 19-1

U.S. AGRICULTURAL COMMODITY EXPORTS TO ASIA, 1994-97

Country	Exports (US$ Bill.)				Share of U.S. Exports (%)	
	FY1994	FY1995	FY1996	FY1997	FY1994	FY1997
Japan	9.33	10.67	11.87	10.70	52.3	45.0
China and Hong Kong	1.99	3.86	3.34	3.40	11.2	14.3
South Korea	2.06	3.58	3.71	3.28	11.5	13.8
Taiwan	2.11	2.56	2.94	2.58	11.8	10.8
Southeast Asia	1.80	2.60	3.37	3.11	10.1	13.1
South Asia	0.55	0.98	0.73	0.73	3.1	3.1
Total Asia	17.84	24.25	25.96	23.80	100.0	100.0
World	43.86	54.63	59.79	57.26		
Asia vs. world (%)	41	43	43	42		

Source: FAS, USDA.

110

of Hong Kong to China in 1997, China moved to the head of these secondary markets, with 14.3 percent, followed by South Korea and the five Southeast Asian countries at 13.8 and 13.1 percent, respectively. Between 1992/93 and 1997, the value of U.S. agricultural exports has grown fastest to China/Hong Kong (26 percent average annual increase), then in the Southeast Asian five (20 percent), Korea (12 percent), and Taiwan (7 percent) (Table 19-2).

Moreover, by 1997, China had overcome the grain shortages that had plagued it in 1995, causing sharply increased imports; instead, it had bumper grain crops, resulting in lower than usual imports in 1997. In the unlikely case that China and Southeast Asia sustain recent high import growth rates, China would overtake Japan as the largest U.S. market in Asia by 2004, and Southeast Asia would overtake Japan by 2008. More likely, however, Japan will remain the largest U.S. market in Asia until roughly 2010, with China and Southeast Asia very close behind.

The main determinants of agricultural import growth are the level and rate of income growth, rate of population growth (and particularly of urbanization), and the trade, agricultural, and investment policies of importing countries. Southeast Asia can be expected to continue to be the fastest growing market area, followed by the Four Tigers (Hong Kong, Singapore, South Korea, and Taiwan), plus Vietnam, China, and India (Table 19-3).

Emergence of a large middle class is a key indicator of the critical income levels at which per capita food consumption increases markedly. The middle class ranges from 23 to 29 percent of the population in Thailand, Malaysia, Singapore, the Philippines, and China. The proportion of the population that is middle class is a congruent indicator of urbanization, which recent studies have found to be closely correlated to increased per capita consumption.

TABLE 19-2
**GROWTH OF U.S. AGRICULTURAL EXPORTS TO EAST
AND SOUTHEAST ASIA,
1992/93 AND 1997**

Country	Value (US$ Mill.)		Avg. Annual Change (%)
	1992/93	1997	
Japan	8,422	10,700	6.2
China and Hong Kong	1,355	3,400	25.9
South Korea	2,121	3,280	11.5
Southeast Asia*	1,507	3,110	19.9
Taiwan	1,958	2,580	7.2

*Indonesia, Malaysia, Philippines, Singapore, and Thailand.

Source: USDA.

TABLE 19-3

**RECENT ANNUAL GROWTH RATES AND ESTIMATES TO 2010
IN 12 KEY ASIAN ECONOMIES (%)**

Country	1996	1997	1998	Forecast 1998–2010
Four Tigers	6.7	6.0	5.0	5.8
Hong Kong	5.0	5.2	2.5	5.0
Singapore	6.9	7.8	4.0	6.5
South Korea	7.1	5.5	− 1.9	5.8
Taiwan	5.7	6.8	6.0	6.0
ASEAN	7.4	5.2	− 5.0	6.5
Indonesia	8.0	4.6	−10.0	6.3
Malaysia	8.6	7.8	2.5	7.5
Philippines	5.7	5.1	2.5	7.0
Thailand	5.5	0.4	− 6.0	6.3
Japan	3.8	1.0	0.3	2.5
China	9.7	8.8	9.0	7.5
India	7.5	4.7	5.0	5.5
Vietnam	9.3	8.0	n.a.	6.5

Source: Author's estimates.

PROSPECTS FOR U.S. AGRICULTURAL TRADE WITH CHINA

Expected rapid income growth is China's strongest claim for U.S. farm and agribusiness attention over the coming decade. However, at least partially countering this attraction are two soft negatives and a hard one. China's per capita income levels remain low, even though they double every 9 to 10 years, and population growth is comparatively low. But most seriously, China has policy and political objections to importing food, particularly from the United States. It tends to treat the United States as the supplier of last resort.

Even so, there is a particularly important reason to pay close attention to China as an agricultural producer and market. By its sheer size, China can have an extraordinarily large and volatile impact on global markets. It is capable of causing a doubling (or halving) of world grain prices and import demand in a single year, as it did in 1995 with a 21 million metric ton increase in its net grain imports. Thus, China can dramatically affect the value of U.S. exports globally for good or for ill in the short term, even without changing its imports from the United States. The volatility of its domestic food output and net food availability can cause or exacerbate its trade volatility. This volatility in turn results from a distressing array of domestic policy and political variables, as if its annual weather and water problems were not erratic enough. Looking longer term, growing import demand from China alone is likely to cause a historic and beneficial reversal, even if only slight, in the 40-year decline in the international terms of trade between agricultural and industrial goods. It could even cause the use of land for agriculture to become increasingly competitive with other uses, helping to stem the worldwide tide of land diversion away from agricultural uses.

What, then, are the prospects for China as an agricultural market? Its net food balance is now on a thin edge, with output easily susceptible to falling behind demand growth. Even beyond its annual plague of concurrent droughts and floods, many other factors jeopardize China's ability to expand output, including growing water shortages, erosion and conversion of land to urban, industrial, and infrastructure uses, and some adverse and even perverse cultivation practices. Each year China loses an estimated 0.5 percent of its arable land to erosion and use conversion.[1] These losses are exacerbated by government policies that emphasize food production self-sufficiency over economic and cost efficiency, that impose state control and administrative measures rather than reliance on market forces, that stress urban labor and industrial and state enterprise problems over rural and agricultural ones, and that maintain state controls over land that often undercut tenure-based incentives for farmer investments. In 1996, the government aggravated the likely costs and distortions of the self-sufficiency policy by making its 27 provincial governors responsible for balancing food supply and demand within their individual provinces. Concern is growing among foreign experts that China's overdependence on administrative measures is causing unsustainable agricultural practices, including the overuse of fertilizer and water and undesirable cultivation practices.

The potential for expanding production derives mainly from opportunities to raise China's comparatively low per hectare (ha) productivity through expanded irrigation, better cultivation practices, and improved seed selection and distribution. Unfortunately, current policies seem to undermine incentives for improving productivity. China's leaders appear to respond to many agricultural sector needs mainly when grain problems become critical and demand attention for political reasons. Nevertheless, the U.S. Department of Agriculture (USDA) optimistically projects a 1 percent average annual expansion in China's food production against an annual population expansion of about 1 percent (13 million people a year).

Even if USDA's assessment proves accurate, China would still have to expand imports by enough to satisfy increases in per capita consumption related to an average per capita income growth of 6 to 7 percent per year. This would mean that grain imports would exceed 30 million metric tons by 2005 (Table 19-4). Forecasts by some groups run higher. In any event, continued high volatility in China's agricultural trade can be expected as it moves in and out of the world market with little warning, attempting to use its state trading monopolies to leverage the best terms for its large exports or import demands.

Figure 19-1 shows the volatility of U.S. exports to China and the low U.S. share of the market. The sharply higher U.S. share in 1995 and to a degree in 1996 resulted from substantial shortfalls in China's grain crops in

TABLE 19-4

CHINA'S AGRICULTURAL IMPORTS, 1996/97 AND 2005/06 (PROJECTED)

Commodity	Imports (Mill. Metric Tons) 1996/97	Imports (Mill. Metric Tons) 2005/06	Increase (%)
Corn	2.0	11.8	490
Wheat	12.0	18.2	52
Rice	0.9	1.1	22
Poultry	—	0.6	—

Source: Frederick W. Crook, *The Future of China's Grain Market* (Washington, DC: ERS, USDA, 1997).

FIGURE 19-1

U.S. AGRICULTURAL EXPORTS TO CHINA: TOTAL AND AS A SHARE OF ALL CHINESE AGRICULTURAL IMPORTS, 1980-96

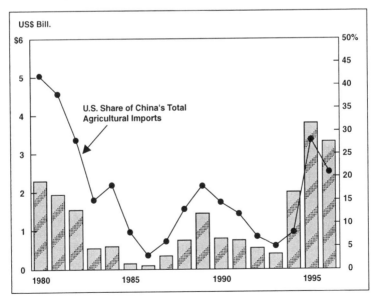

Source: USDA.

1995 and from China's tendency to treat the United States as a residual supplier. The share will probably decline below 20 percent following bumper grain harvests in 1997.

The most important positive change in the prospect of expanded agricultural production in China would occur if China modifies its severe policy of grain self-sufficiency. That would permit producers to shift to more labor-intensive, high value-added commodities such as fruits, melons, meats, and vegetables, each of which has potentially lucrative urban and export markets. With the proceeds of high-value food exports, China could more than pay for expanded imports of land- and water-intensive agricultural commodities that it produces less cost-effectively, such as food grains and feed grains. Even now, part of the challenge to policymakers in sustaining grain output comes from the attraction for farmers of shifting to production of high value-added vegetables.

BEST U.S. STRATEGIES FOR THE CHINA MARKET

Private Sector Strategies

The volatility and politics of China's agricultural market pose moderately high risks for U.S. commodity exporters and agribusinesses. Reliance on export of bulk commodities entails the greatest risk as long as it is China's policy to treat grain imports generally—and those from the United States in particular—as a last resort. For the United States, which already supplies two-thirds of world corn exports, corn ranks as the most favorable commodity for marketing to China because of the rapid growth expected in China's protein consumption and related feed requirements. China's corn imports are projected to reach 11.8 million metric tons by 2005, a five-fold increase over the mid-1990s. Another positive strategy is to focus on the processed and consumer-ready food sector, which leapt from roughly $45 million and less than 10 percent of U.S. exports to China in the early 1990s to $480 million and 23 percent by 1996. Although soybean and other vegetable oils dominate in this category, U.S. exports of consumer-ready products also jumped nine-fold to nearly $100 million by 1996.

Yet another strategy is to acquire market position through direct investment in China; it often involves lower risk, easier market access, and better near-term sales prospects. Processed foods, feed, fruit juices, commodity storage, and bulk transportation and handling are attracting major U.S. agribusiness investments. China is able to leverage its fast growing middle income market to attract investments for processing local agricultural resources. Investments in improved seed varieties and advanced technologies are inhibited by lack of intellectual property law and enforcement. However, opportunities appear favorable for businesses with environmental technologies aimed at achieving more sustainable agricultural practices. Another promising strategy is to seek opportunities associated with cooperative ventures supported by multilateral aid and financial programs, foreign universities, and other nongovernmental organizations.

U.S. Policy Strategies

U.S. and Chinese agricultural economies have great natural complementarities. China is poor in agricultural land, water, management, and technology, whereas the United States is comparatively rich in all four, but lacks low cost farm labor. The potential benefits for the two countries from exploiting their comparative advantages through trade, investment, and other cooperative efforts dwarf those of any other two major economies. The economic advantages from cooperation for both China and the United States would be enormous. China could gain U.S. investments in essential infrastructure for transporting and handling its feed and grain imports and its production surpluses and in value-added facilities for storage, packaging, and processing. China could also gain improved seed and genetic and other technologies. The United States could gain substantially expanded exports of water- and land-intensive crops, especially grains and oilseeds.

The obstacles are mainly political—such as China's grain self-sufficiency aims and its inadequate protection and enforcement of intellectual property rights and U.S. suspension of its investment guarantee and investment feasibility study programs in China in 1989. China's accession to the World Trade Organization regime, possibly in 1999, would greatly accelerate progress toward reducing and eliminating the main barriers to the mutual enjoyment of these advantages.

NOTE

1. China states that it reclaims more land annually than it loses, but it is not clear whether the "new" arable land is as productive and as sustainable for cultivation as the land being lost to agricultural uses. It may depend on expansion of irrigation to new areas.

20

Forecasting China's Demand for Grain

by T.C. Tso

*Chairman of the Board,
Institute of International Development and Education
in Agriculture and Life Sciences, Inc.*

Two key terms should be clarified in discussing China's grain situation. First, the definition of grain in China includes both food grains and feed grains (with rice measured as unhusked paddy rice), legumes, and root crops. Second, grain demand includes four levels—subsistence, above-subsistence, near well-to-do, and well-to-do—each of which is expressed as an amount of grain, in Chinese terms.

THE PAST HALF-CENTURY OF AGRICULTURAL DEVELOPMENT

Between 1949 and 1978, China made little progress in agricultural modernization. In 1965, for example, China's grain production was 195 million metric tons, per capita grain production was 268 kilograms, and per capita food grain consumption was 183 kg. The nation was at the subsistence level, although there was no hunger. In the past two decades, China made remarkable progress in the agricultural sector, mainly due to reforms in, and reversal of, pre-1979 structure and policy, such as abolishing the commune system and reverting farm management decisions to households, reinstating material incentives, and permitting limited free markets and private enterprises. However, this progress can be considered significant only when it is measured against the low 1978 base and the minimal development between 1949 and 1978. If China is to move to a more advanced stage of economic development and to narrow the gap between it and the West by 2000, further basic changes in policy and structure must be initiated.

GRAIN PRODUCTION IN THE NEXT 30 YEARS

In 1986, grain production reached 392 million metric tons, almost double the 1965 level. Per capita grain production was 364 kg, and per capita food grain consumption was 253 kg, the highest levels in Chinese history. The mid-1980s also marked the beginning of China's demand for more feed grain. China reached the above-subsistence level in 1986 and is moving toward the near well-to-do stage. In both 1984 and 1990, per capita grain production was a record 393 kg; the average between those years was 382 kg.

Looking toward 2030, when the Chinese population is expected to peak at 1.6 billion people, three grain scenarios are possible:

- production reaches 650 million metric tons, satisfying a projected per capita need of 406 kg, the near well-to-do level;

- production reaches only 582 million metric tons, or 364 kg per capita, maintaining the above-subsistence level of 1986; or

- production reaches only 429 million metric tons, or 268 kg per capita, the subsistence level of 1965.

Keep in mind that in 1995, China's grain production was 465 million metric tons and that the target for 2000 is 500 million metric tons. Comparing 2030 with 1995, grain production would have to increase by 185 million metric tons to reach the near well-to-do scenario or by 117 million metric tons to reach the above-subsistence scenario. Or it would have to remain at 465 million metric tons to maintain at least the subsistence level. The projection of 650 million metric tons of grain demand in China in 2030 agrees with calculations of outside experts of 479 million metric tons based on conventional Western definitions. There is also a general consensus that China's population will peak at 1.6 billion in 2030. The basic question is, can China be agriculturally self-sufficient by that time?

CONCERNS AND ISSUES

China was alarmed when Lester Brown predicted that by 2030 China would need to buy 216 million metric tons of grain on the world market (292 million metric tons in Chinese terms),[1] especially considering that in 1993, the total international grain commodity trade was only 200 million metric tons. Brown calculated a 1 percent reduction of arable land per year, so that by 2030, grain production in China would be only 263 million metric tons (357 million metric tons in Chinese terms).

Three important factors affect grain problems in China: population, arable land and water resources, and policy.

Population

Since the late 1970s, when a strict family planning policy began, China's population growth rate has gradually slowed and is now under control. The highest growth period was 1951-73, when the average annual increase exceeded 2 percent. Between 1991 and 1995, the five-year increase rates were 1.29, 1.16, 1.15, 1.12, and 1.06 percent. As this slowdown continues, population will peak at 1.6 billion in 2030 and then begin negative growth.

Arable Land and Water Resources

It is agreed that general economic growth has led to shrinking arable land. Chinese official statistics reported that from 1983 to 1994, arable land decreased 10.2 million hectares (ha) or 10 percent. During the same period, 6.7 million ha of land were reclaimed, but the productivity of the newly reclaimed land is only one-third to one-fifth that of the lost arable land. Another significant change is that land productivity showed signs of deterioration during this period. That may be due to factors such as poor management, high chemical input, high cropping indexes, and increased pollution. On the more positive side, total arable land area has been underreported by as much as 25 to 40 percent over the years. Therefore, even taking into consideration an annual reduction of 0.7 percent, the available arable land in 2030 should be much more than is currently projected.

Shortage of water seems to be more serious than shortage of land. With more than 51 percent of arable land irrigated, China has more irrigated land than other countries. However, as China enters the next century, the use of surface water and underground water will reach a limit. In 1980, producing one ton of grain required 1,149 cubic meters of water. By 2000, the projected per ton grain need will be 969 cubic meters, and by 2030, 867 cubic meters. Based on a demand of 650 million metric tons of grain for 1.6 billion people in 2030, 564 billion cubic meters of water will be needed for grain alone. China's total water reservoir capacity was only 475 billion cubic meters in 1994. Considering that more than 70 percent of the Chinese population are in rural areas—farming families, off-farm businesses, and town or village enterprises—the water need for field irrigation, rural society, and households will be 896 billion cubic meters. If water for industry and urban families is included, total water demand will be well above 1,000 billion cubic meters by 2030. How can these land and water problems be solved?

Policy

The major policy issues involve marketing systems, land ownership, science and technology, and total input or investment in agriculture, including infrastructure. The current marketing system is not "free"; it includes quotas, price restrictions, limitations on commodity movement, and various forms of taxation. Farmers have the right to use the land only within an assigned period; there is no ownership. As a result, farmers do not want to invest in the land they till. In 1995, government investment in agriculture was less than 0.7 percent of agricultural gross domestic product. In 1996, investment in agricultural research and education was only 0.19 percent of agricultural GDP.

REQUIREMENTS TO ACHIEVE SELF-SUFFICIENCY

Self-sufficiency in agricultural terms does not mean producing everything in need, but producing to full capacity in accordance with ecology and natural resources, using trade and commerce to satisfy the remaining need. The requirements to achieve self-sufficiency in 2030 are discussed next.

Arable Land

Although arable land was lost at a rate of 0.7 percent per year from 1983 to 1994, total arable area decreased only 0.3 percent a year because of the addition of newly reclaimed land. A careful evaluation of the pattern of land loss by a Chinese scholar revealed a four-stage process in an "S-shaped" curve: flat, peak, valley, and flat again. These ups and downs are closely associated with changes in society's fixed capital investment. If China's future economic growth is less than 10 percent a year, total annual arable land loss will be only 0.14 percent (annual loss of original arable land would be below 0.4 percent). Based on this pattern, China can maintain 90 million ha of arable land in 2030—81 million ha of original arable land and 9 million ha of reclaimed land.

Considering that the multiple cropping index is 1.556 and that food grain occupies 74.8 percent of total sowing area, the calculated food grain area is thus 1.16 times the total area. On that basis, China could have 105 million ha of food grain production area by 2030. Further assuming an average yield of 6,200 kg/ha, China could reach a target of 650 million metric tons of grain. That target is achievable because:

- Total arable land area is currently underreported by 25 to 40 percent; because the actual area is higher, the reported grain yield is inflated. This provides more potential for further increases in grain production.

- Modern science and technology, including biotechnology, new seeds, better pest control, and improved field and postharvest management, will significantly increase yield, reduce waste, and improve utilization.

Water

Increasing water use efficiency, reducing evaporation loss and waste, and developing new water resources may provide some solutions to growing shortages. At present, to produce 650 million metric tons of grain, the water needs, including evaporation, would be 658 billion cubic meters. Considering that water transportation efficiency is 30 to 40 percent and that field crop water use efficiency is 60 to 70 percent, it should be possible to find ways to reduce the loss of water. Developing water conservation practices and searching for new water resources are urgent needs.

Policy

Between 1978 and 1983, China gradually abolished the commune system. The positive effect is that farmers have the right to use and manage their farms. The negative effect, as noted above, is the separation of land ownership and land use—the state, not the tiller, owns the land. Farmers thus have little motivation to protect the land. Their only objective is to squeeze more out of the land. Further, the government policy, the "Three Highs," encourages farmers to manage the land without regard for natural resources and conservation. Under these conditions, farmers have no interest in preventing soil erosion and water loss or in increasing land productivity; they use little or no organic fertilizer; and they have no incentive to invest in improving the land or in protecting long-term resources.

In grain marketing, the government fixes the price and restricts the sale location. Generally, farmers' interests are sacrificed to protect the interests of urban residents.

These policies must be changed. Only through change can farmers be encouraged to produce more and to earn a better livelihood.

FUTURE GRAIN DEMAND

As China continues its economic growth, there will be continuous demand for better living conditions and a better quality food supply. China has great potential to produce sufficient grain to feed itself, either at the near well-to-do level or at the above-subsistence level. China's grain demand will not cause a world grain shortage, or "world hunger," in 2030 or beyond.

China will continue to import grain for several reasons. Among the nine agricultural regions in China, five have a surplus and four have a deficit in grain supply. It is sound logistics and economics to import grain in the east and southeast coastal areas where the population is dense. Importing grain to coastal cities substantially eases the burden of transportation, of storage facilities, and of distribution systems. In addition, it reserves more food in the inner areas.

As dietary preferences change and nutrition improves, China will need more feed grains, and feed grain demand may be much higher than food grain demand. As the economy grows, per capita grain demand may exceed the 400 to 500 kg level, which also will increase the amount of imports. Under the current situation of total government control, the level of grain imports to China cannot be predicted by population or societal needs. There is considerable elasticity between above-subsistence and well-to-do levels. By 2030, imports of 50 million or even 100 million metric tons of grain, for both food and feed, is a completely reasonable prospect.

NOTE

1. Lester Brown, *Who Will Feed China? Wake up Call for a Small Planet* (New York: Norton, 1995.)

PART VI

POLICIES TO AID U.S. FOOD AND AGRICULTURAL TRADE AND INVESTMENT IN ASIA

21

The Impact of Recent Trade Agreements

by Robert H. Curtis

Director, Agricultural Trade Office,
American Embassy, Milan, Italy

I n East and Southeast Asia, increasing per capita disposable income is driving demand for food and consumer products. Demand growth is much greater than production gains in these countries. Therefore, the question is not will trade to this area expand, but how much will it expand, and what are the opportunities for the United States?

U.S. agricultural exports to Asia increased from about $16 billion in 1993 to about $24 billion in 1997. Currently, the Pacific Rim countries account for more than 60 percent of U.S. exports. Even excluding Mexico and Canada, more than 40 percent of U.S. exports go to the Pacific Rim, and by 2000, 50 percent are projected to enter these markets. Yet there is a wide annual variability in the demand for U.S. agricultural goods in the Pacific Rim, depending on China's production. If China has a good corn or wheat crop, obviously its imports will fall and its exports may increase as well, competing with the United States.

ROADBLOCKS TO TRADE EXPANSION

A major question is what will happen to trade if both production and consumption are expanding and a significant number of xenophobes in each country try to restrict trade as much as possible? Some officials want to restrict trade because they are afraid of anything that is imported. In South Korea, for example, there are continual programs and policies against imports. It is amazing that South Korea has displaced Mexico as the third largest U.S. export market. Even so, South Koreans have a perception that imported food and food products are of poor quality and are to be avoided. Agribusinesses need to continue to promote the high quality of U.S. produce, which is superior to the produce that most consumers in Asia can obtain from their local market.

One factor limiting the growth of U.S. sales in the Asian market is the lack of a cold storage chain from the port to the producer. In the Pacific Economic Cooperation Council (PECC), Carole Brookins, Chair and Chief Executive Officer of World Perspectives, Inc., has been diligent in promoting refrigeration seminars to stimulate awareness at the consumer level as well as the business level. South Korea erects many barriers in this area. Shelf-life restrictions on sausages are an example. Korea wants only sausages that are frozen to be imported. Initially, these were required to come in one month after they were produced in the United States, which is less time than it takes to manufacture and ship the product overseas. The basis for Korea's decision is that most of the Koreans who live outside of Seoul do not have refrigerators or freezers; they might take home thawed sausages in which the bacteria count had started to rise. Even though the validity of that rationale is questionable, the Koreans believe it and use it to restrict U.S. imports.

IMPLEMENTING CURRENT AGREEMENTS

Trade agreements are the basis of most of U.S. export growth. Although market promotion, export credits, and export enhancement programs may be important in promoting exports, trade agreements are essential to that growth. Exporters must have access. In Asia, current and future multilateral and bilateral trade agreements will provide export opportunities to ensure that this market continues to grow for the United States.

Negotiating multilateral and bilateral agreements can be tedious. The Uruguay Round of the General Agreement on Tariffs and Trade (GATT) took eight years to negotiate, but a good agreement emerged. One of the most important changes was the provision of market access. Each market must meet a minimum access, which provides U.S. export opportunities that will continue to increase. The United States has derived additional benefits from the Uruguay Round that include increased sales of rice to Japan and oranges to South Korea.

Most of the countries that negotiated the Uruguay Round have fulfilled their obligations, but two major countries, the Philippines and South Korea, are behind schedule. There are opportunities in the Philippines for U.S. exports of poultry and beef. However, the Philippines will allow only fresh beef imports. Obviously, the United States cannot export fresh beef to the Philippines because of the time it takes to ship it, unless it is shipped air freight, a prohibitively costly undertaking.

South Korea has gone to great lengths to restrict imports by manipulating tariff-rate quotas (TRQs) and using nonscientific standards to regulate products coming into the country. It also has very slow import clearance procedures. The United States will continue to address these issues on a multilateral and bilateral basis.

FUTURE ACCESSION TO THE WTO

/Taiwan and China, among the largest 10 export markets for the United States, want to accede to the World Trade Organization (WTO), as do Vietnam, Cambodia, Nepal, and Tibet. They realize that the future of trade and security in the world lies with this multinational group. Each additional country in the WTO means increased market access, trade promotion possibilities, and trade opportunities for the United States. It will probably be the major supplier to these six countries once they become part of the WTO.

] China has been engaged in a multiyear struggle to join the WTO on its own terms. China believes that the WTO should let it in merely because it is a large, powerful economy. The process of WTO accession is not simple. For example, during the process, any member of the WTO can challenge any trade practice of the candidate country. That country must comply with WTO rules and regulations even if it means changing the structure of its domestic economy. This is a major problem for China, as it is for Vietnam and Cambodia. Membership in the WTO is unanimous; if one member says "no," the candidate must discuss with that member how it can gain its vote.

/The United States has serious reservations about China's compliance with the WTO. The state trading system allows China to hide export subsidies as well as to adjust market prices not only in its own market but also in the international market. China has high tariffs, and it has inconsistent sanitary and phytosanitary (SPS) rules and regulations. The list is long. China is such a large producer and consumer of food and agricultural items that its potential to negatively impact international trade is immense if it is simply allowed in the WTO. In one year, China could decide that it was going to influence, or destroy, the price of corn, for example, and it could flood the market if it had an abundant corn crop. This could be accomplished with export subsidies, over which the United States has no control; it is one of many areas in which China could affect not only U.S. production and trade but also the way of life in the United States.

NONTARIFF RESTRICTIONS ON IMPORTS

Another issue regarding tariffs is that a nation can provide market access for a certain amount of product by establishing a tariff-rate quota and then have excessively high tariffs when that quota is exceeded. Under the Uruguay Round, the United States has a minimum access of 3 to 5 percent of consumption for each product in each market, and that access rises every year, reaching around 7 percent by 2000. Because all products must now have tariffs, countries are looking for other ways to restrict imports. One way is through SPS measures. For 20 years, Japan used SPS measures to keep out U.S. exports of apples, and it is attempting to restrict tomatoes in the same way. However, under the Uruguay Round, all SPS restrictions must be scientifically based. The WTO has created a forum in which to address these issues. The United States is hopeful that Japan will not be able to limit U.S. exports of tomatoes for 20 years.

The United States also has problems with China over SPS issues on citrus and fruit, stemming from a 1992 agricultural agreement between the two countries, and with Australia for its restrictions on fruit, pork, and poultry. When South Korea again began to use its trade-distorting shelf-life requirements to limit trade, the United States took that issue to the WTO and won the first agricultural case considered by that body. Another issue with South Korea is its requirement that 100 percent of imported fresh fruits and vegetables be inspected, even though it is unnecessary to inspect each container and box that is imported. The United States has again taken South Korea to the WTO in an attempt to modify these inspection procedures.

RECENT SUCCESSES FOR THE UNITED STATES

The United States has been successful with a number of bilateral trade agreements, such as the Japanese apple agreement noted above. In addition, Taiwan recently reduced over 400 tariff lines after several years of negotiation, and Thailand cut tree nut tariffs from 50 percent to 10 percent.

The United States is exploring a bilateral trade agreement with Vietnam, although the most effective way to deal with Vietnam may be through the WTO. Vietnam and Cambodia will be niche markets for some major U.S. exporters, especially for fruits, grains, and animal genetics. However, because of their population size, disposable income, and economic structure, these countries will probably never be major traders with or major markets for the United States.

Hong Kong and Singapore are obviously major markets for the United States. They are especially important because of transshipments to Association of Southeast Asian Nations (ASEAN). Transshipments to Cambodia, Laos, and other countries to which the United States does not ship directly may now be possible.

THE IMPORTANCE OF APEC

The rest of the ASEAN region will be influenced by what occurs in the Asia-Pacific Economic Cooperation group. APEC has incredible potential. Its broad objective is to sustain growth in the region through trade liberalization, business facilitation, and economic and technical cooperation. The Pacific Rim, which accounts for 60 percent of U.S. exports, is basically APEC. Its 18 members include Mexico, Canada, and Chile, as well as the United States. APEC members are the major trading partners of the United States in Asia and Latin America. APEC is a consensus body; it acts if all members agree. Australians, Canadians, and Americans sit with Japanese, South Koreans, and Chinese. Typically, one side supports more trade across the board, and the other side is more cautious, pushing for only a few changes. Even though the members have such diverse viewpoints, APEC has an agreement in which there will be free and open trade among all the developed member countries by 2010 and with all member countries by 2020.

In the past, agriculture was not dealt with in APEC because the major rice-importing members (China, Japan, South Korea, and Taiwan) did not want the United States to have a forum similar to the WTO in which to discuss opening markets. But APEC decided to address food issues, and a task force is reviewing food supply and demand in the region over the next 5, 10, and 20 years. It is looking at marketing techniques, including how to improve marketing so that exporters can get their products into any country.

Another advance is that PECC, in cooperation with APEC, has developed a trade facilitation manual, based on a survey of the 20 PECC members. For each country, it explains how to get a product in, whether an importer needs a license or a broker, how to obtain tariff information, and how to determine the TRQs. It lists who to contact, the location of offices, and fax numbers. For small and medium-size companies in particular, this manual provides major assistance in their entry into the export world.

Since APEC was created in 1988, it has become increasingly involved in issues worldwide. It will have a major influence in the next multilateral negotiating round of the WTO. In fact, members want to ensure that APEC guides the next round, rather than the European Union and the United States. As a member of APEC, the United States will make sure that its ideas are expressed.

NEXT STEPS

The Uruguay Round is in force until 2000. In 1999, country schedules will again be negotiated, although not from scratch. Initially it was thought that the main elements would continue to be discussed and that export subsidies, internal supports, and tariffs could be reduced, with TRQs increased. However, it is difficult for the United States and the European Union to commit to further reducing their export subsidies when other countries maintain marketing boards and state-trading enterprises that can hide or disguise their subsidy programs. The TRQ administration initially seemed easy and straightforward, but it has proved to be more difficult. Some countries auction import rights to companies, which leads to the creation of monopolies. South Korea gave the TRQ import authority to Korean citrus producers, which is the equivalent of the United States telling Florida tomato growers that they can set the quantity and quality of Mexican tomato imports.

One of the next steps is to study technical barriers. Some barriers are legal under the WTO, such as packaging and labeling rules and regulations, pork clearance procedures, and licensing and certification requirements. However, working out the details will be complex.

22

USDA Export Promotion Activities

by Christopher E. Goldthwait

*General Sales Manager, Foreign Agricultural Service,
and Vice President, Commodity Credit Corporation,
U.S. Department of Agriculture*

East and Southeast Asia are filled with long-term opportunities for U.S. agricultural exporters, traders, and investors who stay committed. Once the regional financial crisis that began in 1997 settles down and Asia begins its recovery, food import demand growth will grow substantially. As a result, Asia's status as a premier growth market for U.S. exporters should be restored.

FACTORS ENCOURAGING U.S. AGRICULTURAL TRADE IN ASIA

Eight important factors make this region one of the most promising markets for U.S. agricultural products.

1. Rapid income growth. Until the crisis in 1997, economic growth rates in East and Southeast Asia were often double to triple the growth rates of most developed countries, and new-found prosperity was broadly distributed. This strong growth created millions of new jobs in the region. As an expanding middle class took advantage of higher incomes, demand for imported meat and poultry products, fruits and vegetables, and processed foods and beverages rose sharply.

2. Trade liberalization. The Uruguay Round of the General Agreement on Tariffs and Trade (GATT) and the future accession of China and Taiwan to the World Trade Organization (WTO) will lower barriers and boost import demand by stimulating economic growth. The Uruguay Round agreement could boost U.S. exports to the Pacific Rim by $3 billion by 2000.

3. Large and growing populations. The population of the Pacific Rim is expected to reach 2 billion people by 2000, and because of its limited arable land, the region is already a net agricultural importer. It will become more reliant on imported food and fiber in the 21st century.

4. Increasing urbanization. Especially in developing countries in Asia, more people are moving from rural areas in search of better, higher paying jobs, creating a ready, accessible market for processed and imported foods.

5. Changing food tastes. Rapid growth in U.S. fast-food outlets and Western-style restaurants and modern supermarkets has contributed to changing dietary patterns. Lifestyle changes, including travel to the United

States, more education in U.S. and other Western universities, and the pervasive influence of Western music, movies, and media, especially on younger consumers, have reinforced the rising demand for U.S. consumer foods. The growth of modern supermarkets has created a more efficient distribution system for a wider variety of imported consumer foods and the opportunity to conduct in-store promotions. In China, for example, supermarkets did not exist until a few years ago; now, new supermarket chains are springing up in most major urban areas.

6. *The increasing prevalence of home appliances.* Refrigerators and microwave ovens give an increasing number of Asian consumers the opportunity and incentive to alter shopping and purchasing habits from the traditional daily trip to a wet market for fresh local products to the less frequent trip to the supermarket for products that can be stored and easily prepared in the home. In China, an estimated 75 to 80 percent of residents in major cities now have refrigerators, which are smaller than U.S. models but often have large freezer sections. Japan is second only to the United States in the percentage of households with microwave ovens.

7. *Better transportation and port facilities.* Improvements in shipping times, port capacities, air transport facilities, and refrigeration technology help assure the quality and timely arrival and storage of U.S. exports to Asia.

8. *Growth in the Asian food-processing industry.* Asia's food processors are increasingly looking to the United States for low cost, high quality ingredients to increase their profitability. The U.S. food-processing industry is well known for its competitiveness, level of efficiency, and pace of innovation to respond to changing consumer demands.

These economic, demographic, and social factors are among the reasons why U.S. agricultural trade and investment in East and Southeast Asia boomed in the early to mid-1990s, though it has since slackened with the economic weakness these countries are experiencing. U.S. agricultural exports to Asia increased from $15.8 billion (37 percent of total U.S. agricultural exports) in 1993 to $23.6 billion (41 percent of the total) in 1997. Over the next decade, exports to the Pacific Rim are expected to rise faster than those to the rest of the world and account for more than 50 percent of U.S. agricultural exports.

EXPANDING USDA's OUTREACH EFFORTS

To ensure that U.S. success in the export market continues, the Foreign Agriculture Service (FAS) of the U.S. Department of Agriculture (USDA) has expanded its domestic outreach efforts. Steps taken by the FAS to inform U.S. exporters, traders, farmers, and businesses of the agricultural export opportunities available to them include:

- establishing an FAS Home Page on the Worldwide Web so that thousands of U.S. exporters have more timely access to FAS information on trade, programs, services, and market opportunities (the FAS Home Page is located at http://www.fas.usda.gov);

* placing FAS employees on temporary duty in strategic locations around the United States, such as in Des Moines and Sacramento, to help the entry of small and medium-size companies, cooperatives, and new-to-export businesses into the export market;

* improving FAS linkages with traditional customers, such as export program participants, cooperators, and state and regional groups, and reaching out to potential new players, such as grower and processor cooperatives, food industry associations, universities, the media, farm groups, and youth groups;

* activating the Attaché Education Program, in which recently returning foreign service officers can make presentations at meetings and export seminars to highlight trade opportunities and avenues to capitalize on new markets and demand for new products.

FAS is also realigning its overseas resources. It has opened an agricultural affairs office in Hanoi and an agricultural trade office in Jakarta to complement the existing agricultural affairs office. FAS has also expanded its agricultural trade offices in Tokyo and Seoul.

These efforts are inextricably intertwined with USDA export assistance programs and trade policy efforts. Together they ensure that the robust pace of U.S. agricultural export sales continues to grow around the world.

EXPORT ASSISTANCE PROGRAMS

The export assistance programs of USDA are designed to introduce, maintain, and increase sales of U.S. agricultural products abroad. They benefit U.S. exporters, traders, and investors, and many activities are geared toward the important Asian market. These programs received welcome support from the farm legislation passed in 1996.

One example is the Market Access Program (MAP), formerly the Market Promotion Program, a cost-share partnership with the U.S. export community. It has been invaluable in helping U.S. producers, exporters, and companies boost sales of high value food products in all types of markets.

The Federal Agriculture Improvement and Reform (FAIR) Act of 1996 authorized MAP at $90 million annually for Fiscal Years 1996 through 2002. During the 1997 program year, 52 percent of MAP funding was allocated to the Asian Pacific Rim markets. In Japan, for example, 38 MAP participants conducted market development activities valued at $27 million. In other markets such as Hong Kong with 25 participants, MAP activities were valued at $6 million, and in South Korea with 28 participants, MAP activities totaled $5 million.

Successes under this program in which the U.S. export community and government work together include: a 22-percent increase in exports of California pomegranates that set new records in 1996; the opening of a new market for U.S. thoroughbred horses in South Korea; and a dramatic apple export expansion to Indonesia totaling $34 million in U.S. exports for the

1995/96 marketing year, and increasing another 10 percent during the first six months of the 1996/97 marketing year.

The Foreign Market Development (FMD) or "Cooperator Program," another export promotion program, is a partnership operated on a cost-share basis with the U.S. export community and U.S. farmer organizations. It allows the programs to pool technical and financial resources to initiate and carry out a variety of foreign market development projects. Federal support focuses on participant expansion into areas of the world where the greatest market development potential exists, including the emerging markets of Asia. During the 1997 program year, 43 percent of FMD funds were allocated to the Asian Pacific Rim markets. Japan was targeted by 24 cooperators totaling $5 million in FMD funds, China was targeted by 21 participants totaling $3 million in FMD funds, while 20 cooperators aimed their FMD projects at Korea totaling $2 million in allocations.

Successes under this program include the elimination of a longstanding nontariff barrier on U.S. graded lumber to Japan, increasing the number of U.S. mills that can export directly to Japan from 80 to 1,000, and an expansion in U.S. poultry exports to China from about $34 million in 1995 to $60 million in 1997. In addition, the U.S. export market for soybean meal in Thailand has nearly doubled in a single year under the FMD program, increasing U.S. exports from 79,000 tons in FY1996 to 151.4 million tons in FY1997.

Export-Credit Guarantee Programs

Other tools for building and expanding export markets for U.S. agricultural products are USDA's export-credit guarantee programs. These programs make it easier for many foreign buyers to obtain the commercial credit necessary to purchase U.S. farm commodities by reducing the risks for U.S. exporters. The GSM-102 Export-Credit Guarantee Program provides coverage for credit periods of up to 3 years, and the GSM-103 Intermediate Export-Credit Guarantee Program covers credit periods of more than 3 years, but not more than 10 years.

In FY1997, GSM-102 export-credit guarantee allocations totaled about $4 billion, and registrations were $2.8 billion for 28 countries and 7 regions. In FY1998, allocations increased to about $5.8 billion for 22 countries and 12 regions. Registrations under these allocations exceeded $4 billion in FY1998.

In 1998, GSM-102 allocations were increased largely in response to the Asian financial crisis. Credit guarantees have helped keep U.S. products flowing to Korea and Southeast Asia, while providing these countries with needed access to key commodities. For example, as of August 7, 1998, FY1998 allocations for Korea totaled about $1.5 billion, compared to allocations of about $154 million in FY1997. Sales registrations under these allocations for Korea totaled about $1.3 billion for fruits and nuts, meats, corn, soybean meal, cotton, soybeans, wheat, hides and skins, and wood products. A regional program has also been introduced in Southeast Asia in 1998, as well as new programs in Malaysia, the Philippines, and Thailand. Allocations continue at FY1997 levels for China, and allocations for Indonesia have been increased by about 35 percent.

In FY1997, GSM-103 export-credit guarantee allocations totaled $373 million, and registrations were about $63 million for 10 countries and 1 region. FY1998 allocations, as of early August, were $310 million for 12 countries and 2 regions. Registrations under these allocations totaled about $51 million. Allocations included $10 million for breeder livestock to Indonesia and $2 million for breeder livestock to the Philippines.

In addition to GSM-102 and 103, new credit tools have been introduced to help U.S. exporters expand, maintain, and develop markets for U.S. agricultural products when commercial financing may not be available without a U.S. government payment guarantee.

The Supplier Credit Guarantee Program is expected to be especially helpful in expanding sales of high value products to some Pacific Rim countries. Implemented in FY1996, this program is designed to help U.S. exporters sell processed and consumer-ready foods to foreign buyers on short-term credit of up to 180 days. It guarantees payment by foreign buyers to U.S. exporters under the terms of a standard promissory note. In FY1997, Supplier Credit Guarantee allocations totaled $105 million, and registrations totaled about $3.74 million for five countries and six regions. FY1998 allocations, as of early August, were $293 million for nine countries and six regions. In the Southeast Asia region (Indonesia, Malaysia, Singapore, and Thailand), Supplier Credit Guarantees have been used for exports of fresh fruits, meats, tree nuts, and solid wood products.

The Facilities Guarantee Program, another new credit tool, helps address infrastructural barriers overseas by supporting projects to improve the handling, marketing, distribution, and storage of imported agricultural and food products. For example, a U.S. exporter might apply for these guarantees to obtain credit to invest in a new port refrigeration facility that would receive U.S. frozen foods in a developing Asian country. In FY1998, $155 million in Facility Guarantee Program coverage was announced for three countries and three regions, including $40 million in coverage for the Southeast Asia region.

Programs to Counter Unfair Trade Practices

Two USDA programs are intended to help counter unfair trade practices of competitor countries by providing bonuses to U.S. exporters for specific commodities and countries. The Export Enhancement Program (EEP), implemented in 1985, was used aggressively for a decade to bolster U.S. exports of wheat, feed grains, rice, vegetable oils, frozen poultry, and eggs. However, because of world market conditions and greater restraint in the use of grain export subsidies on the part of the European Union, USDA stopped offering EEP bonuses in 1995.

In May 1998, U.S. Secretary of Agriculture Dan Glickman reactivated the EEP to announce a 20,210-ton allocation of frozen poultry to six countries in the Middle East to partly compensate U.S. poultry producers for markets lost in Europe. As of early August 1998, 1,500 tons of frozen poultry had been sold under this initiative. Also in May 1998, USDA announced an EEP initiative for 30,000 tons of barley to Algeria, Cyprus, and Norway in response to the European Union's heavily subsidized sales of barley to the United States. Bonuses of $1.2 million were provided for 25,000 tons of barley exports before this initiative expired. In both instances, the EEP was used in a limited and targeted way to address specific unfair trade practices.

In June 1998, USDA announced new one-year EEP allocations for wheat, wheat flour, barley/malting barley, barley malt, rice, vegetable oils, frozen poultry, and eggs. However, except for the still-open invitation for bids on frozen poultry to the Middle East, none of these allocations were made operational. While recent use of the EEP has been very limited, it remains an important tool, and USDA is prepared to use it when conditions warrant to protect U.S. producers and exporters from unfair competition. Congress authorized up to $150 million for EEP bonuses in FY1998.

The Dairy Export Incentive Program (DEIP), which operates on a bid-bonus system similar to the EEP, provides bonuses to U.S. exporters of dairy products. The program has been fully funded for maximum use within the volume and spending limits consistent with U.S. obligations as a member of the WTO. The current DEIP, announced in June 1998, authorizes bonuses for export sales of 84,212 tons of nonfat dry milk, 5,003 tons of whole milk powder, 29,854 tons of butterfat, and 3,350 tons of cheese through June 30, 1999. As of early August 1998, bonuses exceeding $30 million were paid for exports of more than 27,700 tons of nonfat dry milk and nearly 2,600 tons of whole milk powder and cheese. Since 1995, USDA has targeted Pacific Rim markets under the DEIP, and these efforts are paying off. Asian markets have accounted for 20 percent of U.S. nonfat dry milk sales over the past few years.

While some USDA programs help U.S. exporters face tough competition in specific markets, others are aimed at aiding developing and emerging markets with the long-term view of spurring economic growth and prosperity. The PL 480 Title I and Food for Progress programs are primarily tools to alleviate hunger through concessional sales or food donations to needy countries, but they also create an avenue for establishing a U.S. agricultural presence in developing countries, such as those in East and Southeast Asia. History has shown that as developing countries move from low to middle income status, they become growth markets for U.S. agricultural exports. Japan is an example of this transition, but it is not the only example. Today, 4 of the top 10 markets for U.S. agricultural products were once food aid recipients. In FY1998, USDA has provided $290 million worth of food assistance to 25 countries, one of which is the Philippines.

Research, Exchange and Technical Assistance Activities

Research, scientific exchanges, and technical assistance programs are also mutually beneficial to the United States and Asian nations because they promote cooperation and collaboration. Over the years, the Asian countries have benefited considerably from U.S. public, academic, and private industry agricultural expertise. Examples include the development of agricultural universities in India patterned after the land grant university system in the United States. In addition, the International Cooperation and Development (ICD) Program of USDA has helped educate thousands of Asian agriculturalists in U.S. universities and has delivered training courses in specific agricultural disciplines in Asian countries. Since 1978, over 1,100 scientists have participated in scientific exchanges under the U.S.-People's Republic of China Agricultural Agreement. During this time, the program has helped to improve the productivity and the sustainability of agriculture in both China and the United States. Through these exchange and technical assistance activities, the United States has obtained valuable new varieties of germ plasm, biocontrol agents that are native to Asia. This scientific cooperation over the past 50 years has helped improve the research, quarantine, conservation, agribusiness, and pest control capabilities of the Asian nations, as well as those of the United States.

The Cochran Fellowship Program brought more than 100 individuals from Asia to the United States in 1997 for short-term training that included supermarket management, food safety, plant and animal quarantine, and livestock nutrition programs. Training provided through the Cochran Program helped improve foreign specialists' understanding of U.S. practices. A recent initiative has been an assessment of cold chain (i.e., frozen and chilled food distribution system) needs in Southeast Asian countries that will serve to increase importation of U.S. high value products.

ICD coordination with the Natural Resource Conservation Service, the Cooperative, State, Research, Education, and Extension Service, and the U.S.-Asian Environmental Partnership has led to the establishment of an Animal Waste Demonstration Center in Taiwan with new technologies in waste management applicable to Asian countries and U.S. farms.

Another technical assistance program, the Emerging Markets Program (formerly the Emerging Democracies Program), was authorized by the FAIR Act to assist U.S. exporters in emerging markets. Its aim is to foster increased exports of U.S. agricultural products, especially value-added commodities, to improve the effectiveness of food and rural business systems in emerging markets, to address potential reductions in trade barriers, and to increase prospects for U.S. trade and investment. Under the program, an emerging market is defined as one that has a per capita income of less than $8,355 and a population greater than 1 million. This definition will allow the United States to retarget this valuable program to build on its export efforts in several Asian countries such as China, Indonesia, the Philippines, and Vietnam.

The FAIR Act authorizes this program at $10 million a year for the next seven years and requires that $1 billion of direct credit or credit guarantees be made available to emerging markets during FY1996 to FY2002. For FY1997, FAS committed $3.3 million for projects and activities in Asia that include developing an infrastructure for distributing fresh fruit in Indonesia, assessing the softwood lumber market in the Philippines, and developing a market for U.S. high value products in the hotel/tourist sectors of China and Vietnam.

In addition to being used in particular regions, activities of the Emerging Markets Program can be multiregional in scope and complement other export assistance programs or help assist in the resolution of trade policy issues. For example, FAS will use Emerging Markets Program funds to assess proposed projects for the newest credit tool, the Facilities Guarantee Program, and to conduct technical seminars on sanitary and phytosanitary issues.

TRADE POLICY EFFORTS

Trade policy efforts by USDA to open and maintain markets in Asia for U.S. exporters reflect its strong belief that agricultural trade reform must continue if the United States and the world are to benefit from freer and fairer trade.

Although the Uruguay Round brought agriculture more fully under world trade rules, much work remains to be done. The next phase of agricultural trade negotiations under the WTO is set to begin at the end of 1999. These negotiations are U.S. agriculture's best chance for further reducing tariffs, opening new markets, and addressing unfair trade practices on a global scale. Several key issues need to be resolved.

- Substantial further reductions in tariffs are needed. High tariffs in other countries raise costs for U.S. exporters, and many tariffs are high enough to shut the United States out of markets.

- Tariff-rate quotas (TRQs) should be substantially increased or effectively eliminated by cutting the out-of-quota duty. Small TRQ quantities and high out-of-quota duties cap U.S. exports, and restrictive methods of administering TRQs also impede trade.

- Export subsidies should be eliminated. U.S. producers do not need export subsidies to compete as long as other countries are not driving them out of markets with subsidized products.

- Rigorous disciplines should be imposed on the activities of state trading enterprises. In today's economy, there is no justification for monopoly importers or single-desk exporters unless a country is trying to disguise protection or support.

- Tighter disciplines are called for to prevent countries from circumventing their trade commitments through disguised subsidies and nontariff measures. Implementation of Uruguay Round commitments has generally been good, but USDA is uncovering some practices that appear inconsistent with the spirit, and possibly the letter, of WTO rules.

- Rules on sanitary and phytosanitary measures should be more clearly defined and tightened so that countries cannot disguise protectionist intentions. USDA wants to ensure that other countries establish measures for biotechnology and food safety on the basis of sound science, and it will oppose any effort to water down current rules.

These measures would stimulate competition, gear production to demand, increase employment, boost investment, and bolster economic growth. In addition, USDA continues to work with China on its accession to the WTO, especially in the area of obtaining market access for U.S. agricultural products. Successful discussions with Taiwan have already been held on its accession to the WTO. In February 1998, the United States and Taiwan signed a bilateral agreement in which Taiwan committed to opening its market at significantly reduced tariff rates to a broad range of U.S. products and to establish import quotas for poultry, pork, potatoes, and variety meats.

From a regional perspective, U.S. representatives continue to work with Asia-Pacific Economic Cooperation (APEC) trade ministers on market-opening initiatives. Despite Asia's economic woes, APEC ministers have reiterated their commitment to liberalization in nine sectors of their economies, including fish and forestry products. Proposals on food and oilseeds are also being developed.

U.S. trade policy efforts to help Asia during its economic crisis include strong support for additional funding of the International Monetary Fund (IMF) and the World Bank. Without this funding, the U.S. capacity to deal with threats to world economic stability could be undermined, leaving the United States unable to preserve markets for its goods and services.

IMF efforts to aid Asian nations have already resulted in economic reforms in Korea that should be positive for U.S. agriculture. In January 1998, Korea began to harmonize its technical standards affecting food imports with international codes, which should increase access for U.S. exporters. Korea is also moving to revise pesticide tolerance levels in harmonization with Codex Alimentarius, which will allow U.S. fruit to enter Korea unimpeded. Korea agreed to eliminate restrictive licensing provisions that could lead to the solution of a number of long-standing access problems for U.S. exporters of items such as corn grits, soyflakes, and peanuts.

In summary, all USDA efforts—from outreach to realigning overseas resources and from export assistance programs to trade policy efforts—are aimed to ensure future trade and investment opportunities for U.S. agricultural exporters, farmers, traders, and investors in the global marketplace.

23

Dichotomies in U.S. Trade Policies

by Dale E. Hathaway

Director and Senior Fellow,
National Center for Food and Agricultural Policy

T here are perplexing dichotomies in U.S. policies toward trade. One is that even though almost all countries in East and Southeast Asia have graduated from U.S. direct foreign development assistance, these programs continue to be in the long-term interest of the U.S. political economy, based on the assumption that growth and improved levels of consumption lead to political stability and aid in democratization. Yet, programs important to the United States as an agricultural exporter will not be carried out by the private sector because individual companies cannot capture the benefits. Further, in an era of scarce resources, it is unlikely that the United States will return East and Southeast Asian countries to the aid list. The focus of remaining aid funds is on a few countries in the former Soviet Union, Central America, the Caribbean, Africa, and South Asia.

WHO CAN PROVIDE ASSISTANCE?

In the absence of any formal U.S. development assistance program, a resultant policy question is how can faster growth and more equitable income distribution be promoted in the Asian economies? Can the programs of the World Bank or the Asian Development Bank be somehow influenced in that direction? There is much to be done, but paid for and carried out by whom? In addition, the developing countries of East and Southeast Asia need more technology and information systems. Because, as noted above, individual U.S. firms are not going to provide these systems, what kinds of partnerships will the U.S. private sector require to undertake them?

Another issue involves related activities domestically. For example, who is responsible for providing information systems regarding the nature and extent of foreign markets on a country-by-country basis, for maintaining these databases, and for making them widely available to businesses and other interested parties? The attitude in the U.S. government has been that if information systems about markets were not valuable enough for businesses to pay for, such systems probably were not important. Therefore, the government has steadily shed much of its domestic data collection activities and those on foreign economies.

CONFLICTS BETWEEN U.S. FOREIGN POLICY AND U.S. TRADE POLICY

The United States has clear policy conflicts that hamper exports to and investment in Asian economies, a problem that could become more acute. One conflict is between U.S. foreign policy and the use of U.S. commercial and economic policies to make other nations behave in ways that comply with U.S. concepts of justice and ethics. This dichotomy is apparent in the human rights activities in the U.S. Department of State, but it is even more conspicuous in the annual renewal of most-favored-nation (MFN) status for China. Renewal hinges on the U.S. President being satisfied with human rights in China. If MFN is not renewed, barriers to imports of products from China will rise sharply. This threat is intended to make China change its internal policies to reflect U.S. objectives.

The threat of removing MFN is a carryover from the Jackson-Vanik amendment to the Trade Act of 1974, an amendment that was aimed at pressuring the former Soviet Union to let Jews immigrate. During the Carter administration, when relations between the United States and the People's Republic of China began, the issues of Jackson-Vanik and immigration were raised with leader Deng Xiaoping. He is reported to have said, "Oh, immigration. We'll give you a hundred million people. When do you want them?" That was the end of the discussion. Even though Jewish emigration from the countries of the former Soviet Union is no longer an issue, Congress is unwilling to overturn this obsolete legislation.

The annual threatened withdrawal of MFN from China is probably the greatest single conflict between U.S. foreign policy and U.S. trade policy. Each year, there is a prolonged period of uncertainty leading to the President's decision, during which time agricultural groups protest withdrawal and human rights groups urge withdrawal. The Chinese become irritated and turn to U.S. competitors. This is not a rational way to discharge trade policy.

So, one of the most difficult conflicts that needs to be addressed in U.S.-East/Southeast Asia relations, perhaps more than with other parts of the world, is between U.S. foreign policy human rights objectives and U.S. economic policy objectives. Most U.S. competitors are far more interested in their own economic policies and in promoting the international competitiveness of their domestic industries than in the internal policies of Asian countries.

ECONOMIC SANCTIONS

The United States has trade policy conflicts in other parts of the world. Even though there is ample evidence that unilateral economic sanctions do not work unless they are imposed by virtually all countries, the United States persists in using them as the foreign policy weapon of choice. Trade sanctions are perceived by the United States as inexpensive weapons that send a signal. Unfortunately, the imposition of a sanction has proved to be expensive for U.S. exporters, and the signal it sends is that U.S. trade policy is inconsistent.

24

The Irrelevance of Trade Policy and Market Promotion for U.S.-Asia Trade

by R. Gerald Saylor

Director, Market Economics,
Deere & Company

Asia's tremendous potential as an agricultural export market for the United States is due primarily to internal forces that have developed in that region rather than to U.S. trade policy or market promotion activities. The latter factors are of minor importance. If Africa had been growing 8-10 percent per year in real terms during the past 15 years, the United States would be focusing on Africa as well as Asia.

PROMOTING ECONOMIC GROWTH

Underlying economic growth has been the main driver behind the rapid increase in agricultural imports in East and Southeast Asia. Given the amount that the United States has spent on market promotion for feed grains, current feed grain exports should be higher than they were in 1981. However, U.S. feed grain exports are actually lower today than they were then. If market promotion expenditures had high payoffs, this would not be the case; corn exports would not have fallen even in the mid-1980s. Other economic factors such as the value of the U.S. dollar, European exports, or Chinese corn production dwarf international trade agreements like the North American Free Trade Agreement (NAFTA) and market promotion activities. While the United States should certainly continue to work in these areas, U.S. agricultural trade in Asia would probably improve if these economies could be encouraged to adopt the successful economic policies of countries such as China and Taiwan.

The same argument applies to the former Soviet Union and eastern Europe. Whether these countries will be competitors or will serve as markets for the United States in the long term will depend primarily on how well they perform economically. If the economies of the former Soviet Union, by becoming more market-oriented or by investing in people or infrastructure, begin to grow at an 8 to 10 percent annual rate, they may ultimately become a significant market for the United States. U.S. efforts to promote general economic growth are much more important in increasing agricultural trade than U.S. participation in international agreements.

PROMOTING WTO MEMBERSHIP FOR CHINA

The United States would have benefited by admitting China to the General Agreement on Tariffs and Trade (GATT) in the mid-1980s rather than continually delaying that decision. The longer that China remains outside GATT, the longer it will be unrestrained by GATT rules. If China were a member of the World Trade Organization, it could be charged when it violated WTO terms and agreements. However, China most likely has more to gain by not having to play by the rules of the game than by being on the inside. In terms of U.S. interests, China's participation in international agreements is clearly preferable to its exclusion from them.

PROMOTING OPEN ACCOUNTING

The next round of WTO negotiations will probably focus on state trading enterprises. The United States will likely argue that these enterprises must have a different function or perhaps be abolished. Other countries will see this as an infringement on sovereignty, whether it is on the import side or the export side. A more effective course of action, one that would be much less confrontational, would be for the United States to argue for open accounting in those systems. U.S. grievances with the Canadian Wheat Board, for example, are not so much that it subsidizes exports but that the United States does not know which exports are being subsidized or the contract that is being entered into on a specific sale. Open accounting would reveal the sales, the grades, and so forth. The United States would be in a stronger position if it argued for open accounting rather than for the abolition of state trading enterprises, an undertaking in which it is unlikely to succeed.

It is important to point out that a unique and independent policy instrument is necessary to achieve each policy goal. For example, if a country has three policy goals such as a 2 percent rate of inflation, a 4.5 percent rate of unemployment, and $100 billion in agricultural exports, then it must have a minimum of three independent policy instruments to simultaneously obtain the three goals. It is apparent that the United States has numerous goals, but few instruments.

25

Japan's Foreign Aid: Some Lessons for the United States

by Christopher B. Johnstone

*Research Fellow,
Asia Pacific Center for Security Studies*

Despite recent budget cuts, Japan remains the world's largest donor of official development assistance (ODA), a status it has held since 1991. In 1997, Japan gave $9.4 billion to the developing world through both bilateral and multilateral channels. France was the second largest donor at $6.4 billion. The United States provided just $6.2 billion, down about 35 percent from the previous year. These figures represent disbursements that meet the Organization for Economic Cooperation and Development's (OECD) definition of ODA. Other forms of foreign aid such as military assistance and trade credits are therefore not included.

The decline of the United States as an ODA donor in recent years has been dramatic, and until recently Japan's leadership position—at least in volume terms—was large and growing. Budget cuts and the declining value of the yen have somewhat eroded the stature of Japan's foreign aid program, but ODA nevertheless remains a prominent part of Japan's international strategy. Overall, Japanese ODA reductions disguise the large volume of funds that continues to flow to countries and regions of strategic priority. Japan's FY1997 package of aid loans to China, for example, exceeded ¥(yen)200 billion (about $1.7 billion) for the first time.

The scale of Japanese foreign aid has attracted considerable international attention, both praise and criticism, but ODA in fact makes up just one component of a broader set of policies and programs known in Japan as *keizai kyoryoku* (economic cooperation). Although these initiatives serve a number of purposes, and are plagued by a variety of problems, they were in essence developed to support the nation's economic and commercial interests, particularly in Asia. The tools employed in this effort are strikingly comprehensive, ranging from foreign aid and other forms of government-sponsored finance, such as lending through the Export-Import Bank of Japan (JEXIM), to training and personnel exchange programs that bolster Japan's human ties with regions of strategic importance.

JAPAN'S ECONOMIC COOPERATION PROGRAMS

Japan's economic cooperation programs in the postwar period have served two primary objectives, and the outlines of a third are becoming apparent. The first objective, and traditionally the most important, was securing access to raw materials. Japan is a resource-poor nation; for example, more than 99 percent of the oil consumed in Japan is imported. Achieving stable access to raw materials, particularly in the energy sector, therefore has historically been a central goal of the nation's foreign policy. Economic cooperation programs were created in part to serve this interest.

A second goal of economic cooperation has been to transplant declining (sunset) industries to overseas locations. This goal has come to the fore since the mid-1980s as Japan's economy matured and came under pressure to shed low-end industries, particularly in the manufacturing sector. Tokyo sought to facilitate this process through government lending and other forms of assistance that improved the investment climate in the developing world.

In more recent years, the outlines of a new strategy in economic cooperation have begun to emerge—using government resources to encourage Japanese participation in meeting Asia's physical infrastructure needs. Although the current economic crisis will slow the pace of infrastructure development, the region's business potential in this sector is massive, and Tokyo is attempting to give corporate Japan an edge on the competition.

In sum, Japan's economic cooperation programs have long been strategic in intent, even if the final results often fall short of the original objectives.

Size and Scale

Japanese economic cooperation programs are massive and, not surprisingly, focused on Asia. Given the region's proximity to Japan, Asia is of strategic significance to Japan in several ways: as a market for Japanese goods and services, as a source of raw materials, and as a site for Japanese investment.

Well over one-half of Japan's bilateral assistance in 1996 was bound for Asia. China and Indonesia, the two largest recipients of Japanese foreign aid—and not coincidentally the two most promising emerging markets in the region—alone received about $1.8 billion. Because these figures represent net ODA disbursements (new commitments minus repayments of previous loans), the data understate the full volume of annual giving to Asia. New loans to China and Indonesia during FY1996, for example, totaled more than $3 billion. Total JEXIM lending during FY1996 was also massive—about $12.4 billion in the form of loans, trade credits, and guarantees. Asia received about one-half of this volume, with China and Indonesia alone receiving almost $4 billion in JEXIM disbursements.

Characteristics

The inclusion of JEXIM programs in a discussion of Japan's foreign aid program may seem peculiar. OECD follows strict guidelines in determining what forms of assistance qualify as official development assistance. By international rules, ODA is distinct from other government financing programs with a more overt commercial bent. Nevertheless, the forms and objectives of Japanese ODA suggest a commercial intent not significantly different from JEXIM lending and other programs explicitly designed to support business interests. These programs are all part of the broader strategy behind economic cooperation.

To be fair, Japan's foreign aid program has undergone a series of reforms over the past 10 years that has brought it more in line with international norms. Traditionally, much of Japanese foreign aid was openly tied to procurement of goods and services from Japan. In other words, an ODA recipient was required to purchase Japanese goods and services during project implementation. More recently, much of Japanese ODA has been formally "untied," opened to contractors of any nationality, although the transparency of the system remains an issue of international concern. But despite these reforms, several characteristics of Japanese ODA illustrate the continuing prominence of commercial interests in the program.

One is the Asia focus of the aid program. The region is relatively prosperous and growing, despite the financial crisis that began in 1997, and many critics suggest that Japan should provide aid to more needy regions of the world. While more than one-half of Japanese ODA goes to Asia, the average among all OECD aid donors is only 25 percent to that region. Japan's aid program is also characterized by a low emphasis on grants; just 37 percent of Japanese ODA is in grant form. The OECD average is about 70 percent, and for the United States it is about 95 percent. The Japanese aid program also stresses construction of heavy infrastructure such as roads, bridges, airports, and power plants—projects that carry lucrative procurement contracts for the companies involved. About 40 percent of Japanese ODA goes for these purposes, compared with only about 20 percent in the OECD as a whole, although the share of this form of aid in Japan's aid program has declined in recent years. In sum, because Japanese ODA retains a heavy element of mercantilist intent, the program deserves consideration in a broader discussion of economic cooperation as a whole.

OBJECTIVES OF JAPAN'S FOREIGN AID PROGRAMS

Access to Raw Materials

An example of the first of the three broad goals of Japanese economic cooperation—securing access to a stable supply of raw materials and natural resources—is the Asahan Aluminum Smelting Facility in Indonesia. This massive project was financed by Japanese aid during the 1970s and 1980s. It combined Japanese foreign aid funds, technical assistance through the aid program, lending from JEXIM, and private financing from Japanese banks to support construction—by Japanese companies—of a facility intended to produce primarily for the Japanese market. In fact, this single project supplied about 20 percent of Japan's aluminum imports during the 1980s.

A more recent example of this form of economic cooperation is the $1.5 billion JEXIM loan in 1995 to finance Japanese construction of two liquid natural gas facilities in Qatar and in Indonesia. Again, the product of these facilities will be exported primarily to Japan. The historical pattern continues to hold: Japanese government sources, in conjunction with Japanese financial institutions, finance projects that are implemented largely by Japanese firms to extract raw materials for export back to Japan.

Transplanting Sunset Industries

The second goal—transplanting sunset industries to locations overseas—has become more important since the 1980s, as Japan's economy matured and particularly as the yen dramatically strengthened after 1985. In just a few years, the yen appreciated from about ¥250 to the U.S. dollar to around ¥130 to the dollar. The exchange-rate fluctuations imposed a severe burden on lower-end Japanese manufacturing industries. In response, the Ministry of International Trade and Industry (MITI) attempted to develop plans to help industries such as electronics, automobile parts, and metal works, which were most affected by the yen's appreciation, to move overseas.

Eventually, MITI devised the New Asian Industrial Development Plan. The plan consisted of three broad phases, combining all the programs of economic cooperation, theoretically at least, into a cohesive whole. According to the plan, Japanese officials would first work with their counterparts in Asian governments, particularly in Southeast Asia, to devise comprehensive development strategies. Selected export industries were targeted for Japanese investment, and structural barriers to the development of the industries were identified. Second, Japanese government officials and consultants recommended specific projects to facilitate the growth of these industries. ODA funds would be used, for example, to support feasibility studies for infrastructure projects that could support the development of targeted industries. Implementation would begin in the third phase. ODA would be used to build the necessary infrastructure, and JEXIM and MITI financing would be used to promote investment by Japanese companies in the targeted industries and countries.

Just how much of the New Asian Industrial Development Plan was actually implemented remains unclear. The scheme was understandably the subject of considerable criticism in the West. Nevertheless, the plan reveals an intriguing underlying mindset; it suggests, at the very least, an attitude about the proper role of government in shaping economic interests abroad that is quite at variance from that prevailing in the United States.

A New Paradigm

The latest phase of economic cooperation features the promotion of Japanese participation in meeting Asia's physical infrastructure needs. The opportunities in this field are immense. Before the onset of the current Asian financial crisis, the World Bank estimated that by 2004 Asia would have to invest $1.5 trillion in infrastructure—power, transportation, and communications—to maintain the high growth rates of the recent past. The task of building this infrastructure is potentially quite profitable. Public resources, through foreign aid, government bond issues, and other tools, have been the traditional vehicle for building basic infrastructure, but the region's needs far outstrip available official funds. The Japanese government has therefore attempted to find ways to use government resources, through the economic cooperation program, to serve as a "pump primer" for private Japanese investment in infrastructure projects.

Few practical demonstrations of the new paradigm exist, but one example is the construction, now under way, of a subway system in Bangkok. ODA funds are building the system's tunnels, while private money, supported by JEXIM and MITI, will be used to procure the cars and operate the system.

The Japanese government is unashamed of the goals behind this emerging form of economic cooperation. A recent government document offers an illustration: "The government of Japan should consolidate the business environment required to encourage the commitment of Japanese infrastructure providers to private sector-led infrastructure development in developing countries. The government of Japan should try to achieve visible economic cooperation that unifies Japanese technologies, know-how, and financial resources."

Obviously rhetoric does not always match reality. Many Japanese aid programs suffer from inefficiency, poor implementation, and corruption. But economic cooperation programs represent an area in which Japanese government activity continues to be massive and strategic, at least in its design. Despite the common American image of a Japan moving away from active government involvement in the economy and becoming "more like us," government programs aimed at promoting economic interests overseas continue to be massive and continue to be accepted by a wide range of Japanese society.

THE ASIAN ECONOMIC CRISIS

The financial crisis that began in Asia in 1997 presents a formidable challenge for Japan's commercial diplomacy. Although many in Japan view their country as the author of the "Asian economic miracle," Washington has accused Tokyo of failing to do enough to help the region through the crisis. The Japanese economy has been mired in a period of slow growth for much of the decade, and conditions have recently worsened considerably. In this environment, Japan's ability to absorb exports from Asia, thereby fueling the region's recovery, is severely constrained. The United States has demanded that Japan do more to rekindle economic growth, and governments across Asia have recently joined in the refrain.

Despite this criticism, however, Japan has done much to help alleviate the impact of the crisis, relying on the traditional tools of *keizai kyoryoku*. Through the International Monetary Fund (IMF) and bilateral channels such as the foreign aid program and JEXIM, Tokyo has extended more than $40 billion in assistance to affected economies in Asia. Japan also announced in October 1998 the creation of an additional $30 billion fund for countries in need, and other packages may be forthcoming. Some of these funds appear to represent restatements of previous pledges, but by any measure Japan's actions are impressive. Perhaps most notable was Japan's short-lived effort in 1997 to create an Asian Monetary Fund (AMF) as a supplement to the IMF. Through the contributions of member countries in Asia, led by Japan, the AMF would have created a pool of up to $100 billion for use in addressing short-term balance of payments emergencies. Although never fully defined, Japanese officials envisioned a nimble, flexible monetary authority that could respond to financial crises more quickly than the rule-bound IMF—and thereby prevent turmoil in one country from spreading to its neighbors. Japan's neighbors in Asia welcomed the proposal, partly out of a desire to avoid the harsh conditions imposed on IMF lending.

U.S. officials, fearing that the new AMF would usurp the IMF's authority, and possibly weaken America's position in Asia, fiercely opposed the concept, and Tokyo ultimately backed down. Still, the initiative demonstrates the methods by which Japan attempts to curry favor in Asia and the continuing importance of economic cooperation as a tool for supporting Japanese interests abroad. This approach clearly has limitations, as the criticism of Japan in recent months demonstrates. Nevertheless, Japan's willingness to extend massive amounts of aid to its neighbors enhances Tokyo's influence throughout the region—and provides a foundation for corporate Japan's overseas expansion.

IMPLICATIONS

What does all of this mean for developing countries and for the United States? First, it is worth noting that Japan's economic cooperation is not necessarily bad for the developing world, even if the programs are designed to serve Japanese economic interests. Asia needs infrastructure, and it will welcome anyone who can provide it. Japanese foreign aid has financed the construction of 46 percent of Indonesia's hydroelectric power capacity; Indonesia is grateful for the assistance, even if Japanese firms profit from the funds. Second, Japan's practices are also not necessarily bad for U.S. business. To the extent that Japanese foreign aid is used to finance roads and railways, U.S. business is better able to get its products to new markets. American firms directly competing in the sectors most supported by Japanese foreign aid, particularly infrastructure providers, may face increased competition, but other companies benefit in a host of indirect ways.

Are there lessons for the American foreign aid program from the Japanese experience? This is a sensitive question. Japan is justly criticized for the commercial focus of its aid program. However, at a time in which international altruism in the form of foreign aid is increasingly out of fashion, Japan's approach has one dominant virtue: Japanese aid practices cultivate a domestic constituency, and in turn political support, for a large foreign assistance program. Business ultimately supports Japanese foreign aid because it understands that benefits flow back to it, although at times corporate Japan complains that its access to the program is inadequate. Therefore, even in a period of increasing budget constraints in Japan, the aid program is fundamentally sustainable. While there is much to criticize in the questionable motives behind Japanese foreign aid, Japan's approach nevertheless raises the question of whether the United States could do a better job of demonstrating linkages between foreign aid and American business interests without compromising the program's quality and objectives. A program closer to the Japanese model would undoubtedly be more self-serving; it might also be more politically sustainable.

26

The U.S. Stake in International Agricultural Research and Development

by Earl D. Kellogg

Associate Provost, International Affairs, and Professor, Agricultural and Consumer Economics, University of Illinois at Urbana-Champaign

T o a considerable extent, the economic future of U.S. agriculture lies with increasing agricultural exports and advancing effective trade policies. Developing countries, which already capture more than 50 percent of U.S. agricultural exports, will continue to play a large role in that future. However, other international factors will affect the economic future of American agriculture as significantly as exports and trade policy. Thus, a broader strategy for promoting U.S. agricultural interests in the future should be developed.

A BROADER STRATEGY FOR U.S. AGRICULTURE

The United States will have many global challenges to address in the next several years. How can the nation ensure that its agricultural interests continue to be protected and promoted in a complex, interdependent world? In addition to export demand and trade, several issues are important to the future health of U.S. agriculture.

First is the international dimension of agricultural research and technology dissemination. A key factor in the competitiveness of U.S. agriculture will be the effectiveness of the U.S. research and technology development system and the U.S. ability to access knowledge and technology developed outside its borders. The amount and quality of foreign research relevant to U.S. agriculture is increasing rapidly, and the United States must find avenues, particularly in the public sector, in which to responsibly participate in this process. Substantial technology flows back to the United States from agricultural research, and technology development systems abroad can contribute to the strength and vitality of U.S. agriculture.

Second, U.S. agriculture has an enlightened self-interest role to play in international development. The sector needs to influence the type of development that is occurring and how it affects U.S. interests.

Third, the United States must seriously consider human capital. Is the United States developing individuals who can effectively lead the country in the next few decades? Competition for world markets is intensifying. Are there rising leaders who understand what is happening in marketing, business organization, and scientific innovation at home and around the world?

Capitalizing on International Agricultural Research

The United States needs links to international agricultural research systems. For example, there are 13 international agricultural research centers operating in more than 30 developing countries under the aegis of the Consultative Group on International Agricultural Research, a donor consortium. The annual budgets of those centers are fairly small, $200 million in total, but they are developing technology and knowledge that have direct relevance to U.S. agriculture. However, U.S. connections with this international research system are waning. A decade ago, 9 centers were led by Americans; today, there are only 2. The United States should concentrate on accessing the international scientific community, particularly in the developing world.

The Australian attitude toward international agricultural research is instructive. In an effort to understand how Australia could benefit from agricultural research under way in other parts of the world, several years ago the Australians brought together members of their Parliament, leaders of the Australian agricultural sector, Australian scientists, and leaders of the international agricultural research system. The theme of the conference was, "What is being done in the international research system that makes a difference for Australia and Australia's agriculture?" The United States should consider similar avenues for an in-depth exploration of the international agricultural research community, particularly in the public sector.

Encouraging Broad-Based Development

The broad-based development that has been under way in East and Southeast Asia is the result of years of investing in people, institutions, and other resources and of making tough policy decisions. This kind of development is in the best interest of the United States, even given the recent setbacks some of these economies have suffered in the financial crisis.

Because the United States supports various bilateral and multilateral development institutions, it should be involved in defining the kind of development they are promoting. Broad-based development increases the incomes of poor people and encourages the growth of a middle class. Such development requires, among other factors, sound macroeconomic policies in these countries. In addition, agricultural growth and rural nonfarm employment must be encouraged. For most low income countries, agriculture is such a large sector that overall economic growth is not possible without agricultural growth. This fact places the United States in a paradoxical position—to promote U.S. agriculture's interest in developing countries, the United States must promote agricultural development in them. U.S. agriculture must not only be involved in defining what is good for the country in foreign assistance, but it must also undertake such aid more purposefully than in the past.

Broad-based development can have a substantial impact. In the 1970s and 1980s, Asian countries such as South Korea, Thailand, and Malaysia experienced rapid growth in their gross domestic product and agricultural sectors. Not only did their economies and agricultural production grow, but they also had substantial agricultural exports. That scenario might seem to suggest that they did not have large agricultural imports. But this was not the case. Agricultural imports and exports both expanded rapidly as economic development progressed. The United States supplied a significant portion of their imports. When such broad-based economic growth occurs, it can generate a powerful demand-expanding system.

It is revealing to compare the total value of foreign assistance to the value of exports in these countries. For example, from 1946 through 1992, the total U.S. foreign assistance to South Korea amounted to $14 billion. Today, the annual value of U.S. exports to South Korea exceeds $14 billion. Annual U.S. imports to all of the countries of East and Southeast Asia (except for Indonesia) exceed total U.S. aid in the past 50 years. While the focus is often on how much money the United States spends on foreign assistance, it should be kept in mind that aid has a high return in terms of increased exports to countries experiencing broad-based growth.

Training People for the International Agricultural Marketplace

Finally, how can the United States increase human capital to meet the challenges of an increasingly complex global future? Some years ago, I received a phone call from a Japanese agribusiness leader about a young man from Japan who had applied to the University of Illnois's graduate agricultural marketing program. He asked if the student was going to be admitted, and I said the student's records were strong enough for admission, but not for financial support. He responded that the young man was a corporate employee, so the company would pay any tuition involved.

Then he added that he did not want the student overloaded with courses every semester. I replied that the student would have to finish the master's degree within a certain period of time, but that if he were careful he could pursue his coursework a little less intensively and still get through.

I asked the caller why he was interested in a reduced course load. He told me that his company was investing in the student for the long term. He wanted the student to understand U.S. agricultural markets. He wanted him to go to Chicago to learn about the Board of Trade and the Mercantile Exchange. He wanted him to get to know people in the business and to learn how to play golf. He also wanted him to have time to understand American humor, and he hoped the student would become a good social mixer.

The businessman told me that he had done the same thing at the University of Illinois 20 years earlier. He said that for 20 years his company had been investing in sending Japanese students to U.S. universities to learn about the United States, U.S. agriculture, and U.S. business and social systems.

How many U.S. young people are in Japanese universities? How many are in Thai universities, in Malaysian universities, or in Indonesian universities?

CONCLUSION

An increasingly complex and interconnected world requires U.S. agriculture to think broadly about its interests in the future. The agricultural sector must be concerned about exports and trade policy because these variables affect agriculture's well-being in the short and intermediate term. Also profoundly affecting the United States in the future will be the effectiveness of the U.S. agricultural research system and U.S. efforts to become an integral part of the international research system. The United States should be aware that this country's degree of success with development efforts to improve the well-being of low and middle income people in developing countries will be a powerful determinant of future demand for U.S. agricultural products. U.S. agriculture thus has a substantial stake in the type of development being encouraged around the world. Another important element for determining the future is how well the United States develops agricultural leadership to understand and help shape the globalization of agriculture.

27

The Impact of Development Assistance on U.S. Trade with Asia

by Charles F. Weden, Jr.

*Former Deputy Assistant Administrator,
Bureau for Asia and the Near East,
U.S. Agency for International Development*

T here are organizations such as the Heritage Foundation that say the watchword for economic development should be "trade, not aid." They claim that if poor countries could only get their economic policies right, including an open trade regime, growth would follow. They cite pre-financial crisis Asia as an example of how well this formula can work.

Some of these assumptions are correct, but not the central conclusion. Trade is important to economic growth, and proper economic policies are crucial. There is ample evidence to support the importance of these two factors. For example, from 1970 to 1989, the 15 developing countries that maintained open policies grew at an average of over 4 percent a year, while 74 developing countries that did not liberalize or had mixed economies grew by only 0.7 percent a year. The Heritage Foundation is correct that pre-crisis Asia offers good examples of a model growth formula, but not the formula that the foundation had in mind. Examples are South Korea and Taiwan—two of the Four Tigers and both, it should not be forgotten, former recipients of substantial U.S. Agency for International Development (USAID) assistance. The watchword should more properly be "aid, then trade."

Ultimately, private investment must drive the engine of lasting economic development. But something more fundamental has to take place first. Emerging markets do not arise automatically. Countries do not automatically develop sound economic policies, even if they have mustered the political will to bring about change, nor do they simply start importing U.S. goods and services because they are developing open trade regimes. A nation has to reach a certain level of development before it can become a good customer of U.S. exports.

SOME FORMER AID RECIPIENTS

USAID contributed to the economic development of South Korea and Taiwan, though clearly much of their success prior to the recent Asian financial crisis had to do with a strong Confucian work ethic, a reverence for education, and a propensity to save. In addition, both countries benefited from the stability gained through a U.S. security presence. However, USAID assistance surely was pivotal to the successful development of both countries.

Between 1949 and 1965, Taiwan received $1.7 billion in U.S. economic assistance. During a somewhat longer period, South Korea was the beneficiary of approximately $5 billion of U.S. aid. That assistance had many dimensions, but USAID played a particularly important role in three areas.

First, USAID trained the cadre of leaders necessary to bring about successful development. Literally thousands of individuals in Korea and Taiwan were trained in nation-building skills during the 1950s and 1960s. It was not coincidental that when a critical mass of these skills was in place, the economies of South Korea and Taiwan began to move.

Second, USAID helped establish the economic policies that created the successful growth model. The South Koreans and Taiwanese then took over the policy reins. Initially, both countries favored protectionist import-substitution policies. In both cases, it was USAID that persuaded them to adopt their now heralded export-led strategies.

Finally, USAID supported, and indeed initiated, South Korean and Taiwanese efforts to bring about balanced development. This meant, for example, that urban industrial development was balanced with equitable rural development and that population growth and health concerns were factored into development planning to achieve sustainable development (USAID initiated family planning programs in both South Korea and Taiwan). Concern for the environment and democratic institutions was not part of USAID's mandate at that time, and South Korea's and Taiwan's progress in these areas was stunted until relatively recently.

The rest is history. Today, South Korea and Taiwan are large markets for U.S. exports of primary products, mainly food and fiber.

U.S. DEVELOPMENT ASSISTANCE IN ASIA TODAY

After 30 years and about $1 billion in USAID assistance, Thailand has "graduated" from aid recipient to aid donor and has been helping its close neighbors, Laos, Cambodia, Vietnam, and Burma. USAID's role in Thailand was similar to the role it played in South Korea and Taiwan. USAID is working with the soon-to-be Tigers, Indonesia and the Philippines, with South Asia's newly accelerating economies, India, Bangladesh, Nepal, and Sri Lanka, and with the transitional economies, Mongolia and Cambodia.

These nations, which include the bulk of the region's population, possess tremendous economic potential, despite the mainly short-term effects of the Asian financial crisis. Most are moving toward market economies but are not yet assured of sustained growth. Nearly all are dogged by the global challenges of population growth, environmental pollution, and the growing pandemic of HIV/AIDS. Nearly all are attempting, with varying degrees of determination, to bring about more representative, transparent government, without which their continued stability cannot be assured. Finally, all are well disposed to the United States and look to USAID as the principal source of technical assistance for achieving sustainable development and more representative government.

But much else has changed. For example, the United States is no longer the leading donor in Asia, or even a major one. The top three donors are Japan, the World Bank, and the Asian Development Bank. In 1996, in several Asian countries, USAID ranked as the sixth or seventh largest donor after the European Union, Germany, and other European donors. Obviously, the United States welcomes increased assistance by others in Asia. But is it ceding the field? If so, what impact will this have on the U.S. leadership role in Asia? How will this serve U.S. long-term interests?

Since 1990, U.S. economic assistance to Asia has fallen by more than 65 percent. Part of the decline is due to the successful completion of USAID's Thailand program, the termination of assistance to countries like Pakistan and Burma, and the completion of USAID's contribution to special activities such as the Multilateral Assistance Initiative in the Philippines. Even after allowing for these factors, however, the drop-off can only be characterized as precipitous.

Due to the decline in resources, USAID has made hard decisions to preserve the best of its programs while attempting to retain the influence developed over the past 40 years. In allocating its resources, USAID has looked carefully at factors such as assistance activities that make the strongest contributions to U.S. foreign policy objectives, USAID's comparative advantages in providing assistance, what other donors are doing, and, of course, what the governments and the recipients in assisted countries want USAID to do, as well as the degree of their commitment to these programs.

Despite the decrease in resources, USAID retains considerable influence with host governments in the region and with other donors. This is due partly to USAID's long-term presence and partly to the on-the-ground expertise of resident USAID missions. But mostly it is because USAID is providing quality technical assistance in a wide range of important areas, including economic reform, trade policy, environmental protection, population control, HIV/AIDS prevention, democracy, and governance. Other donors provide funding for infrastructure, equipment, relief commodities, and the like, but USAID is Asia's top provider of technical assistance. With the almost universal movement in Asia toward economic and sector policy reform, U.S. advisors are in high demand. As a result, USAID's assistance leverages many times its value in contributions from other donors and in foreign direct investment.

The following list includes examples of the types of assistance that USAID is providing and shows the impact that aid can have.

- Indonesia and the Philippines reduced average tariff rates from around 20 percent to 15 percent, and both countries are scheduled to reduce tariffs to 5 percent by 2004 because of agreements under the General Agreement on Tariffs and Trade/World Trade Organization, the Asia-Pacific Economic Cooperation forum, and the Association of Southeast Asian Nations. USAID trade policy technical assistance to government ministries in these two countries contributed to their willingness to implement these and other trade reforms.

- Indonesia announced in 1995 its intent to eliminate all barriers to the import of soybean meal, and in 1996 it gave substance to that announcement by removing the domestic content requirement for soybean meal. This policy change opened the $200 million Indonesia market for soybean meal imports to U.S. and other soybean exporters. USAID advisors in Indonesia's Ministry of Trade and Industry prepared the studies that helped persuade the government that such a policy change would be highly beneficial to the poultry industry by lowering feed costs.

- Nepal mission's Agro-Enterprise Center successfully brokered a joint venture between Minneapolis-based Universal Cooperatives and a local agribusiness firm for the export of 200 metric tons of Niger seed to the United States.

- In India, agribusiness ventures supported by the USAID mission's Agricultural Commercialization and Enterprise project have attracted $60 million of additional domestic investment into agribusiness activities over the past few years, especially for the production of mushrooms, flowers, and fruit for export. USAID has fostered Indo-U.S. agribusiness linkages that have opened important opportunities for the purchase of U.S. agribusiness equipment, especially refrigeration units, and for joint ventures in biotechnology.

- In the Philippines in the early 1990s, USAID worked with NAPOCOR, the government energy monopoly, to design and implement a Build-Own-Transfer (BOT) plan to obtain private sector financing for new energy plants. To follow up on its success in the energy sector, the BOT program was expanded to other infrastructure sectors including telecommunications.

CONCLUSION

U.S. development assistance in Asia has had a strong impact not only on the development of the region, but also in advancing U.S. interests. Although greatly diminished in resources, this role is still strong. However, U.S. assistance levels in the region are dangerously low. If they fall any lower, the longer-term interests of the United States will suffer.

CONCLUSION

Looking to the Future

by Mark R. Drabenstott

Vice President and Economist,
Federal Reserve Bank of Kansas City,
and Chair, NPA Food and Agriculture Committee

T he Food and Agriculture Committee (FAC) began its study of the Asian market for U.S. food and agricultural products more than two years ago. The chapters in this book are based on presentations made at several FAC meetings. The authors revised and updated in Winter 1998. When the study began, little did we know that the region was headed for a full-blown financial and economic crisis. The near-term challenges are clearly great as this dynamic region tries to regain its economic footing. Notwithstanding the urgency of addressing the region's current economic crisis, the findings presented in this book clearly speak to a much larger long-term issue—helping the region realize its potential as the world's largest food market. While U.S. agriculture is rightly concerned about the policy measures necessary to stem the crisis in Asia, no one should lose sight of the enormous long-term potential the Asian food market represents.

Although the current economic and financial crisis is complex, over the long run the Asian food market will be driven by simple fundamentals. As Carole Brookins points out in Chapter 1, more than 1.5 billion people will leave behind rural dwellings and subsistence agriculture and move to developing Asian cities over the next 25 years. What is more, the region is expected to contain 7 of the world's 10 largest cities by that time. While cities will claim less than half the region's population, a marked move to urbanization points to sharp increases in food demand.

The bigger driver in the Asian market will be income growth. Consumers in the United States are now accustomed to spending only 10 cents of each new dollar of income on food. Asian consumers, on the other hand, are eager to improve their diet, and thus are quite willing to spend 30 to 40 percent of every new rupiah or bhat or renminbi on food. The region will simply not have the food systems necessary to meet this ramp-up in food demand. A huge population eager to eat better spells opportunity for U.S. food and agriculture.

REALIZING THE ASIAN POTENTIAL

The chapters in this book make it clear that realizing this vast potential will not be easy. The current economic and financial crisis must be addressed—not just by band-aids but by putting long-term solutions in place.

This will be an enormous challenge because it will require reorienting government policies, implementing new financial systems and regulations, and fostering new levels of cooperation within and beyond the region among policy officials and private sector leaders. By most estimates, this economic recovery process will require years rather than months.

The hard work will not end once the Asian economy is back on its feet, however. Many pieces must fall into place for the Asian food market to reach its full potential. While many of these will be unique to the region, some will involve public and private decisionmakers in the United States, too.

Trade policy figures to be a critical and contentious issue moving forward. Perhaps the greatest threat of the current economic downturn is the prospect that Asian nations and their trading partners may turn to trade protectionist measures in search of short-term economic relief. Such steps inevitably yield a harvest of shrinking trade, less efficient domestic industries, and even less economic growth. Thus, vigilance against trade protection will be an essential byword over the next few years in keeping the door open to future growth. U.S. agriculture can play a very constructive role throughout this critical period by being a calm, steady voice for freer trade.

Many trade issues will remain even if protectionism is avoided. China will be a growing economic force in Asia, and much uncertainty surrounds its accession to the World Trade Organization (WTO). This issue will certainly impinge on the next round of multilateral trade talks sponsored by the WTO. That round will no doubt return to the thicket of agricultural subsidy issues that were center stage at the Uruguay Round. Market access, export subsidies, and nontariff barriers to trade will get considerable attention, both in the Asian food market and elsewhere. Eclipsing these more conventional issues, however, may be trade in genetically modified organisms. More common ground on intellectual property rights—long a contentious issue in Asian trade—will be a prerequisite to future growth in the Asian food market. A framework that will sustain trade in U.S. genetically modified products and the export of Asian genetic material to the rest of the world will be critical to realizing Asia's market potential.

Infrastructure poses another huge challenge in fostering future growth in the Asian food market. Over the long term, U.S. food exports to Asia may be limited more by infrastructure than by income. China's current infrastructure inadequacies illustrate the problem. China has very limited port capacity, and its rail system simply cannot handle the volume of food and commodities that the United States routinely ships. Thus, Chinese demand for U.S. products could far exceed the ability to deliver products to Chinese consumers. Moreover, one of the biggest problems throughout Asia is the general lack of cold chains—the chain of refrigerated distribution that makes it possible to ship value-added products like meats to consumers in many countries.

Obviously, Asian infrastructure needs to grow along with Asian food demand. For this to happen, the region must have financial systems and an investment climate that inspire the confidence of investors in the region and throughout the world. This only serves to underscore the need for creating resilient financial systems and sound regulatory regimes. With such systems in place, U.S. firms probably will choose to be strong partners in Asian infrastructure investments.

RETHINKING U.S. AID PRIORITIES

Finally, several chapters in this volume show that there is a growing divergence between U.S. food and agriculture's rising stake in the Asian food market and the shrinking role that U.S. development assistance is now playing in the region. Put simply, development assistance has shrunk to a region that promises to be—at least in the case of food and agriculture—the United States's biggest long-term customer. This suggests a fundamental rethinking of aid priorities and the opportunity to play a very constructive role when Asia in general is seeking assistance. Additional development assistance may pay double dividends—helping the region out of its current crisis now and paving the way to a much bigger market later.

Without any doubt, U.S. food and agriculture has an enormous stake in the Asian food market. The region's current economic downturn has been a major factor behind the steep slump in U.S. agricultural commodity prices in 1998. While the near-term problems continue to captivate the attention of public and private leaders, the fact remains that no other region of the world offers more upside potential for U.S. food and agriculture over the next two decades. With careful attention to the sound policy steps discussed in this book, the industry stands an excellent chance of doing well while helping scores of millions improve their diet.

FOOD AND AGRICULTURE COMMITTEE

T he Food and Agriculture Committee (FAC), sponsored by the National Policy Association in Washington, D.C., is a unique private sector group that actively seeks to improve nutrition and alleviate hunger through an open food system. FAC members represent all segments of U.S. food and agriculture—farming, business, universities, foundations, and nonprofit organizations. The Committee's continued emphasis since 1943 on defining common interests and fostering a broad-based consensus from the diverse views of its members has enabled the FAC to become an effective force in the development of national policies and private sector initiatives concerning food and agriculture.

FAC members currently focus on a number of major issues.

- *U.S. competitiveness in an open food system.* As the world's leading trader of food and agricultural products, the United States has much to gain from freer trade and steps to further enhance its competitiveness. The FAC continues to study the effects of liberalized trade on the U.S. farm economy and ongoing efforts to lower trade barriers.
- *The role of food safety* and the link between diet and health present a major challenge and opportunity for the industry. The application, and often resulting controversy, of new production and processing technologies as well as innovations in biotechnology and genetic engineering have increased the urgency of this issue. The FAC examines the many competing and contradictory food safety claims to develop credible information sources that will serve as a basis for policymaking.
- *The relationship of agriculture and the environment* is a priority Committee concern. Actions that protect the environment have important implications for agriculture. The FAC explores these linkages and the ways that environmental and agricultural objectives can be simultaneously achieved.
- *Changes in the structure of food and agricultural markets* have accelerated in recent years with increased concentration, industrialization, and globalization. Advances in technology will likely further revolutionize the structure of these businesses. The FAC continues to study these changes.

FAC members also participate in two subcommittees.

- *Trade, Development, and Global Issues Subcommittee.* This subcommittee focuses on issues that affect the U.S. food and fiber sector as a result of the globalization of world markets for products, inputs, and services used in production and marketing, as well as trade and development issues and policies.
- *Food, Nutrition, and Technology Subcommittee.* This subcommittee examines food production, marketing, and policy issues; nutrition issues as they tie into the food system; and emerging technologies that deal with priority concerns in the food and nutrition complex.

The FAC is completely self-supporting, financed by annual tax-exempt contributions obtained by its members from their organizations.

For further information about the FAC, please contact:
James A. Auerbach
NPA Senior Vice President and FAC Director
National Policy Association
1424 16th Street, N.W., Suite 700, Washington, D.C. 20036
(202) 884-7627   e-mail npajim@npa1.org

MEMBERS OF THE FOOD AND AGRICULTURE COMMITTEE

MARK R. DRABENSTOTT
Chair;
Vice President and Economist,
Federal Reserve Bank of Kansas City

RAYMOND M. CESCA
Vice Chair;
Managing Director, World Trade,
McDonald's Corporation

NELS ACKERSON
Chairman,
The Ackerson Group, Chartered

WALTER J. ARMBRUSTER
Managing Director,
Farm Foundation

SANDRA S. BATIE
Elton R. Smith Professor in
Food and Agriculture Policy,
Department of Agricultural Economics,
Michigan State University

ROBERT H. CALDWELL
Master,
North Carolina State Grange

DAVID CARTER
President,
Rocky Mountain Farmers Union

LARRY D. CASE
National Advisor,
National FFA Organization

RAYMOND R. CASEY
Vice President,
National and Corporate Affairs,
Ohio Farm Bureau Federation

ROBERT CHARLTON
Global Director,
Government and Public Affairs,
DowAgro Sciences

NEVILLE CLARKE
Program Coordinator,
Texas A&M University System

LESTER M. CRAWFORD
Director and Research Professor,
Center for Food and Nutrition Policy,
Georgetown University

LYNN M. DAFT
Senior Vice President,
PROMAR International, Inc.

STEVEN J. DAUGHERTY
Director of Government and Industry Relations,
Pioneer Hi-Bred International, Inc.

MICHAEL DEEGAN
President and Chief Executive Officer,
Agricultural Cooperative Development
International/Volunteers Overseas
Cooperative Assistance (ACDI/VOCA)

F. PARRY DIXON
Director of Economic Research,
Archer-Daniels-Midland Co.

MARVIN DUNCAN
Professor,
North Dakota State University

JACK EBERSPACHER
Chief Executive Officer,
National Association of Wheat Growers

CAROL TUCKER FOREMAN
President,
Foreman Heidepriem & Mager Inc.

RAY A. GOLDBERG
Moffett Professor of Agriculture and Business,
Emeritus,
Harvard Business School

RON G. GOLLEHON
McLean, VA

RALPH GROSSI
President,
American Farmland Trust

NEIL D. HAMILTON
Ellis and Nelle Levitt Distinguished Professor of
Law, and Director, Agricultural Law Center,
Drake University

JOSEPH T. HANSEN
Secretary-Treasurer,
United Food and Commercial
Workers International Union

DALE E. HATHAWAY
Director and Senior Fellow,
National Center for Food and
Agricultural Policy

JOHN JAMES
Senior Vice President,
Pioneer Hi-Bred International, Inc.

DENNIS R. KEENEY
Director,
Leopold Center for Sustainable Agriculture,
Iowa State University

EARL D. KELLOGG
Associate Provost for International Affairs
and Professor of Agricultural
and Consumer Economics,
University of Illinois at Urbana-Champaign

DEAN KLECKNER
President,
American Farm Bureau Federation

LOREN KRUSE
Editor,
Successful Farming

VICTOR L. LECHTENBERG
Dean of Agriculture,
Purdue University

CHARLES K. MANN
Research Associate,
Harvard Institute for International
Development

TERRY L. MEDLEY
Vice President—Biotechnology,
Regulatory and External Affairs,
DuPont Nutrition & Health,
DuPont Agricultural Enterprises

JOHN MILLER
Chocorua, N.H.

ANTHONY C.E. QUAINTON
President and Chief Executive Officer,
National Policy Association

BONNIE E. RAQUET
Vice President—Washington
Corporate Relations,
Cargill, Incorporated

DON REEVES
Policy Consultant,
Bread for the World Institute

THOMAS D. RUGG
Director of Legislative Affairs,
The National Grange

ESTHER RUUD
Agricultural Appeals Mediator

R. GERALD SAYLOR
Director, Market Economics,
Deere & Company

JOHN M. SCHNITTKER
Director of Government Affairs,
Public Voice for Food and Health Policy

SUSAN G. SCHRAM
Deputy Director, Washington Operations,
Food and Agriculture Program Coordinator,
CIESIN (Center for International
Earth Science Information Network)

JEROME B. SIEBERT
Economist,
Agricultural and Resources Economics,
University of California-Berkeley

DWIGHT STIEHL
Executive Vice President,
Rose Packing Company, Inc.

DEBORAH G. STRAUSS
Executive Director, GCRS Inc.,
and Managing Editor, *DIVERSITY*

RICHARD E. STUCKEY
Executive Vice President,
Council for Agricultural Science & Technology
(CAST)

GREGG SUHLER
Program Director,
FAPRI - Missouri

DANIEL A. SUMNER
Frank H. Buck, Jr. Professor,
Department of Agricultural Economics,
University of California-Davis

GENE L. SWACKHAMER
President (Retired),
Farm Credit Bank of Baltimore

LELAND SWENSON
President,
National Farmers Union

ROBERT L. THOMPSON
Sector Strategy and Policy Specialist,
Rural Development Department,
The World Bank Group

RICHARD WAGNER
Corporate Planning Director,
GROWMARK, Inc.

CONNIE M. WEAVER
Department Head and Professor,
Department of Foods and Nutrition,
Purdue University

VERA P. WEILL-HALLÉ
Representative,
International Fund for Agricultural
Development

NATIONAL POLICY ASSOCIATION

T he National Policy Association (NPA) is an independent, private, nonprofit, nonpolitical organization that carries out research and policy formulation in the public interest. NPA was founded during the Great Depression of the 1930s when conflicts among the major economic groups—business, labor, and agriculture—threatened to paralyze national decisionmaking on the critical issues confronting American society. NPA is dedicated to the task of getting these diverse groups to work together to narrow areas of controversy and broaden areas of agreement as well as to map out specific programs for action in the best traditions of a functioning democracy. Such democratic and decentralized planning, NPA believes, involves the development of effective government and private policies and programs not only by official agencies but also through the independent initiative and cooperation of the main private sector groups concerned.

To this end, NPA brings together influential and knowledgeable leaders from business, labor, agriculture, and academia to serve on policy groups. These groups identify emerging problems confronting the nation at home and abroad and seek to develop and agree upon policies and programs for coping with them. The research and writing for the policy groups are provided by outside experts and NPA's professional staff.

In addition, NPA undertakes research and special projects designed to provide data and ideas for policymakers and planners in government and the private sector. These activities include research on national goals and priorities, productivity and economic growth, welfare and dependency problems, employment and human resource needs, and technological change; analyses and forecasts of changing international realities and their implications for U.S. policies; and analyses of important new economic, social, and political realities confronting American society.

In its work, NPA demonstrates two related qualities. First is the interdisciplinary knowledge required to understand the complex nature of many real-life problems. Second is the ability to bridge the gap between theoretical or highly technical research and the practical needs of policymakers and planners in government and the private sector.

Through its policy groups and its research and special projects, NPA addresses a wide range of issues. Not all NPA trustees or members of the policy groups are in full agreement with all that is contained in NPA publications unless such endorsement is specifically stated.

For further information about NPA, please contact:

NATIONAL POLICY ASSOCIATION
1424 16th Street, N.W., Suite 700
Washington, D.C. 20036
Tel (202) 265-7685   Fax (202) 797-5516
e-mail npa@npa1.org   Internet www.npa1.org

SELECTED NPA PUBLICATIONS

Understanding Different Employment Practices, ed. Peter Cappelli. An NAR-commissioned study available from Oxford University Press (1999).

How Public Education Must Respond to Meet the Challenges of a Global Society, NAR Occasional Paper #2, by Donald P. Nielsen (20 pp, 1998, $5.00), NPA #292.

An Agnostic Examination of the Case for Action on Global Warming, NAR Occasional Paper #1, by Murray Weidenbaum (12 pp, 1998, $5.00), NPA #290.

Through a Glass Darkly: Building the New Workplace for the 21st Century, ed. James A. Auerbach (148 pp, 1998, $15.00), NPA #289.

The Inequality Paradox: Growth of Income Disparity, ed. James A. Auerbach and Richard S. Belous (276 pp, 1998, $19.95), NPA #288.

Trade Blocs: A Regionally Specific Phenomenon or a Global Trend?, by Richard L. Bernal (48 pp, 1997, $8.00), NPA #287.

Foreign Assistance as an Instrument of U.S. Leadership Abroad, by Larry Q. Nowels and Curt Tarnoff (32 pp, 1997,.$15.00), NPA #285.

When Earnings Diverge: Causes, Consequences, and Cures for the New Inequality in the U.S., by Richard B. Freeman (80 pp, 1997, $12.00), NPA #284.

Change at Work, by Peter Capelli, Laurie Bassi, Harry Katz, David Knoke, Paul Osterman, and Michael Useem. Commissioned by NPA's Committee on New American Realities (288 pp, 1997, available from Oxford University Press, $27.00).

A Synopsis of Change at Work (40 pp, 1997, $8.00), NPA #284.

U.S. Public Policy and the American Diet, ed. by James A. Auerbach (24 pp, 1995, $5.00).

Food and Agricultural Markets: The Quiet Revolution, ed. by Lyle P. Schertz and Lynn M. Daft, published jointly with the Economic Research Service of USDA (340 pp, 1994, $17.50), NPA #270. Second printing, 1997, with a new Introduction by Mark R. Drabenstott.

An NPA subscription is $100.00 per year. In addition to new NPA publications, subscribers receive *Looking Ahead*, a quarterly journal that is also available at the separate subscription price of $35.00. NPA subscribers, upon request, may obtain a 30 percent discount on other publications in stock. A list of publications will ʼe provided upon request. Quantity discounts are given.

ʼA is a nonprofit organization under section 501 (c) (3) of the Internal Revenue ʼe.

NATIONAL POLICY ASSOCIATION
1424 16th Street, N.W., Suite 700
Washington, D.C. 20036
Tel (202) 265-7685   Fax (202) 797-5516
e-mail npa@npa1.org   Internet www.npa1.org